Finding Happiness In The Face Of Suffering

Adewale Adejumo

Published by Adewale Adejumo, 2022.

While every precaution has been taken in the preparation of this book, the publisher assumes no responsibility for errors or omissions, or for damages resulting from the use of the information contained herein.

FINDING HAPPINESS IN THE FACE OF SUFFERING

First edition. March 11, 2022.

Copyright © 2022 Adewale Adejumo.

ISBN: 978-0620984416

Written by Adewale Adejumo.

Table of Contents

Introduction 1

Take Responsibility 23

Live Your Own Principle 41

Experience Joy In The Face of Suffering 55

Live In A State Of Abundance 69

Owning Less Means Having More 85

The Power Of Habits 95

Set Long-Term Goals 111

Something To Do 121

Meditation 133

Learn As Much As Possible 151

Conclusion 165

Sources 175

Once again. You've picked up a book. Flipped to the dedication page but only to find that the author has once again decided to dedicate the book to someone else, and not you.

Not this time.

We may not have met and may never meet but I trust that we may always think fondly of each other.

This one is for you.

Introduction

No one really sits down to teach us, step by step, the foundations of living a happy life. We go to school, learn Math, Science, Drama, and even how to cook, however, there are no classes for happiness. Why is that? And although we are all born instinctively happy, we grow up, learn and pick up traits, build up ego, and play characters in life that essentially denotes unhappiness. One of my favourite internet quotes by Jim Carrey reads: "Depression is your avatar telling you it's tired of being the character you are trying to play." Unhappiness is often caused by the character we play in life. This book will help you understand some of the philosophical aspects of life. It will teach you how to live a happy life while giving you practical, real-life actions you can take to adopt the trait you need for a peaceful life.

Happiness is one aspect of our lives that not a lot of us are trained in, and in which there are simple skills and principles one can learn to be happy and cultivate joy - just like how we go to school to learn, which then helps us to have the ability to excel in different areas of our lives because we set a goal of finishing the different levels in our education. For example, our Nursery, Primary, Secondary, and tertiary education and so on.

The goal of this book is to have you graduate at the end of it with the skill and knowledge you require to be happy. You could name this "The School of Self". This book is not just about sharing ideas with you, it is more profound and is guaranteed to involve a shift in consciousness. I would like you to experience this shift as you spend time reading, or to deepen your change of consciousness, because you may already be going through this shift in consciousness. This read may be a deepening for you in your change in consciousness. If you have already had your awakening and are living a conscious life of peace, I promise you will not be disappointed by the skills and knowledge you will gain.

Happiness is a goal for most of us in life, no matter your level of success, money, and status. However, suppose you ask most people what their goals are, hardly anyone will say "My goal is to be happy", and because we do not consciously make happiness a goal, we do not do what we ordinarily do when we have a goal, which is to create a plan specific to that goal. A goal must be specific, otherwise, we would end up doing so many things and wonder why we are not getting closer to our goals or reaching them fast enough, which in and of itself, can make us frustrated, sad, and unhappy. The problem with goal-setting is that most people set "means" goals instead of "end" goals. The difference between these two is that end goals define outcomes where you're unwilling to compromise — they describe exactly what you want. Means goals, on the other hand, are just a few of the many paths to reach your end goals.

Examples of means goals are; getting a promotion, starting a business, etc. We then go and attain the skillset either by doing research or studying to help us get to that goal. Most people think they will be happy when they achieve some sort of "means" goals but realise they are still unhappy. They then move the pole to another "means" goal and on and on and on it goes. I am not saying that there is anything wrong with means

FINDING HAPPINESS IN THE FACE OF SUFFERING

goals. Absolutely nothing wrong with them. I just want you to know the difference that means goals are all they are—a means to an end. Means goals are enablers, but if you tie a means goal to your happiness, you will realise—if you haven't already—that happiness will forever be fleeting. Here's the thing: until happiness becomes a conscious goal, and you research the skills to be truly happy, then happiness will always elude you.

Happiness is an end goal, and to understand how to get to an end goal, you need the proper skills, and no, it will not come from the accumulation of things and people. This is because true happiness is an inside job. No amount of external goals will bring you true happiness without you first learning the skills and knowledge of what will bring you true happiness, and that starts inside of you.

You may have noticed that you have been going through your own evolutionary process of growth, it may have been so slow that you may have hardly noticed it. You may have noticed the things that cause you suffering, yet you do them repeatedly. This is not just on your personal level, it happens to a collective—to all of mankind. We repeat mistakes and suffer until we can no longer withstand the suffering, which is always a great point to reach. You may have noticed this happening to you as well because it isn't rare. This is a natural progression for pretty much everyone, to reach that point in your suffering when you can no longer withstand the suffering. The suffering has its purpose. You would not be reading this if you had not had your share of suffering, in fact, I don't think anyone would be reading this if they hadn't had their share of suffering. I have experienced suffering.

Retrospectively, I am grateful for the suffering I have experienced. You should be thankful for the suffering you have and maybe still are experiencing or any suffering to come. Because the suffering has brought the whole of humanity to the point at which we find ourselves today in the awakening of human consciousness and finding our inner peace.

Do you watch space documentaries? Or read books on Astro science? They will tell you about everything that is out there. These documentaries and books are brilliant with their attempts at explaining the wonders and mysteries of the universe, which by the way, is wonderful and filled with plenty of mystery. Yet, we know very little about the universe. Very little! But here's something about the universe that these shows and books about space don't often tell you: that the universe is conscious. How do I know this? Well, I'm conscious, plants are conscious, animals are conscious, and we are all a part of the inner of the universe; hence the universe experiences its consciousness through us. We are the inner consciousness of the universe, right? So, if the universe wants to learn about its consciousness, the universe would look at itself.

Imagine now that you are the universe. Imagine that you want to learn about your consciousness. Where will you look? Inside, isn't it? Your consciousness is inside because it is. How conscious are you of your universe? Do you live in your own universe? Do you truly know how it works? The way you get to experience consciousness is through your body, spirit and mind, that is how you experience consciousness. For you to fully experience your consciousness, you need to understand it and know how it works. A lot of people—just like scientists

FINDING HAPPINESS IN THE FACE OF SUFFERING

that do research—spend so much time looking outwardly that they don't pay enough attention to the inside.

This results in apportioning blame to external factors, self-victimisation; because let's face it, making yourself a victim feels good at that moment and is partially satisfying but the problem of playing the victim is that you stay stuck at that level of consciousness that you are at and life doesn't seem to get better for you, and yet, it feels good to absolve yourself from responsibility. A paradox really, because you want to feel good and become happy, but then you do seemingly absurd things that lead to a conclusion that seems logically unacceptable or self-contradictory because the victim game will not take you where you want to go, which is to possess peace and happiness. This absurdity is as a result of our ego. I am sure you have heard this word "ego" before. I have personally heard it used plenty of times, but I never actually knew what it meant. What is ego? Simply put, your ego is your identity. I will share a little about the ego below, but we will dive deeper into the ego in the up coming chapters.

The ego is generally defined on people who have an exaggerated sense of who they are and believe that they are better than others. That is one aspect of the ego. The other part of the ego is that people have a strong image and self-identify as being a victim of somebody else or others. This works too! This is all as a result of the conditioning of the mind. It's all in the head and from the construct of thought, and this keeps them trapped on the level of their thought and at the level of their personality.

The ego creates perceptions of things and people as soon as they come into your awareness. You label people and things. Yet all of this is a result of the conditioning of your mind. We are unable to remove the veil to see what is beyond the perceptions of our conditioned minds, which is our normal.

The biggest question is: who are you? What is your identity? Is your identity your name? What is your essence identity, your true identity? Can you tell me?

Most people think they know what their identity is, which is the identity they form as a result of their conditioning through comparison of themselves to others. This comparison often results in them thinking they are superior or inferior to others or blame others whenever it is convenient. This type of identity is based on external factors. They form this identity based on things such as the history of their family, their cultures, religions, ancestors and think this makes them more important than the rest of the population. They might even have titles tied to those things and think that's what defines their identity.

To tell you a funny story, I pursued a title to sit on a board of directors of a Non-Profit organisation once. Right after I got my appointment, I went over to LinkedIn and Facebook and updated my new role – "Board of Director" and I received congratulatory messages: "Wooo, aaaah! Well done!". My reason for pursuing this title, as noble as it might sound, was to be in a position where I could make an impact. Still, my ego also felt good because I had attached a part of my identity to this nice big title that earned me praise and recognition from people within and outside my industry. We were all being

FINDING HAPPINESS IN THE FACE OF SUFFERING

played by our egos. Some saw me as superior because of this title. While I'm sure, some saw me as inferior because they have other big titles in bigger organisations to which they belong, or they are wealthy. Some saw me as just what I was: an egocentric asshole that thinks a title will make him feel better, and yet they felt they were better because they do not let labels define them. Yet, these types of people are also egocentric. They are spiritually egocentric. To cut this long story short, I did not get happier, nor did I get any fulfilment from all these external boosts to my ego. It is saddening to realise that a lot of us tie material things and titles to ourselves in search of happiness and to feel a sense of importance.

You may have money, lots of it, which fills you with a great sense of identity. You may have titles, or a beautiful body or looks. You can have all these material things that people chase. When you tie these things to your identity, it will never ever be enough, and some of these things change. Anything that you have that is external, that you think you own, be it money, looks or a partner, I'm talking even of billionaires, all of the things you have are borrowed. One day, you will look in the mirror and notice you are not as beautiful as you once were, or that your body is not as hot as it used to be—even your wealth changes. Nothing external of you is permanent. What are you going to tie your identity to then?

Many people carry uneasy, unhappy personalities with them, and that is how they think they are, but that is not who they are. That is the way in which their minds have been conditioned and the emotions of unhappiness that come with the conditioning of the mind.

You are not your past, and you are not who you think you are as a person. There is more to you than your past and who you think you are as a person. There is more beyond your personality and some of that part of you has already awakened, which is why you are reading this. This goes far beyond your personality and goes into a dimension of your deep consciousness. This dimension of your consciousness has brought you here to deepen your awakening so that you can find peace and start to live a happier life. Finding peace and happiness will occur when you see the world as it comes to be in each and every moment, rather than as you want or perceive it to be.

For the lessons of this book to have an impact on you, you have to keep an open mind throughout but most importantly, you have to take action. Perhaps I should have mentioned that from the beginning, because you may have been reading this entire time and wondering: "What the hell is this guy on about?". You do already have an open mind which is why you are reading this, or you may have been forced to, and you think it's all nonsense before you've even started reading. If you keep an open mind, that's all I need to ensure that after you are finished reading, you will not experience life the same way as you did before. You will have a more profound sense of your identity, and you will walk away, or I should say: put this book away filled with a higher sense of your essence identity and peace. I will recommend that you read this book more than once. Because depending on where you are on your journey to self-discovery, you will miss a lot of very valuable information, which will require you to read this more than once. I have

FINDING HAPPINESS IN THE FACE OF SUFFERING

designed this book to be read at least three times to get the full value from it, as you grow.

The information in this book is about looking within rather than externally. Instead of looking for external happiness, look for it within you. Steven Kotler and Jamie Wheal's book, titled: "Stealing Fire: The Secret Revolution in Altered States" reveals research conducted by numerous scientists that offer shortcuts to happiness through being plugged into machines that will cost you thousands of dollars per session, which many people cannot afford. The book reveals that money can definitely buy short-term happiness - something we already know. The thing is, you don't need to be able to afford these sessions or be plugged into a machine to be happy, unless you have an extreme mental health problem, because you can cultivate your own happiness and increase your happiness without the need for external factors, and in the process, create positive habits while destroying negative habits. However, if you can cultivate your happiness from the inside, and you have money, power, and success, even better. Learning how to cultivate your own happiness is a powerful skill and tool to have because it raises your level of awareness and consciousness which improves your IQ. You will be able to learn other things more quickly once you know and practice the tools and habits of the happiest people in the world. Higher IQ will help you grow faster, solve problems more easily and reach your goals faster. You may hear some motivational coaches say things like: "They are not smart.", "They did not get good grades in school." and: "Yes! I made myself into a success." and all that jazz. Here's the truth: they *are* smart. Smarts is not your ability to store and regurgitate information, being smart is your ability to apply the information you have learnt. Traditional schools really just try to shove so much information down our brains, which does not necessarily translate to living happily or becoming successful in life. I know a lot of people from school with exceptional grades who do not have their lives together, which goes to show that those are not the type of smarts I'm talking about here. The kind of smarts I am talking about here is the type where you understand life on a different level. The smarts that let the world's most successful people achieve massive success in wealth and happiness. These types of smarts will help you reach your external "means" goals that can help you live a very comfortable life. I am telling you this because I did it, and there are millions of people in the world doing this every day.

This book places great value on health and longevity by living a simple life, having inner peace and taking control of your life. At a certain period in my life, I used to party and drink every weekend, I got up to a lot of mischiefs, I would binge-watch shows that added no value to my life, at all. Simultaneously, the world continued to move forward, but my experience was that I was in the same place year after year. In fact, my life felt like it was moving in reverse. I was not able to keep up with my obligations, such as business and romantic relationship obligations, my family, and most importantly, obligations to myself. I exercised perhaps only once every three weeks and had gained weight around my waist and stomach, which made me look part skinny and part fat. I am by no means body-shaming; that is just what I looked like. I had thin arms and a fat waist, thanks to my genes from my Dad. Dad, I see you! The result of

FINDING HAPPINESS IN THE FACE OF SUFFERING

not keeping up my obligations to myself was a failed romantic relationship, a failed business, failed friendships, I did not have a close relationship with my family. I was sad, depressed, stressed, broke, I felt lonely, and on top of that, suffered from anxiety. I should add that by the traditional definition of "smart", I am quite smart. Good grades, high IQ according to classic IQ tests, but I was a failure in life.

While we're on the topic of anxiety, I had anxiety from being around people, from getting into my car because it was not covered by insurance because payments were delayed. I would be anxious receiving phone calls from numbers I didn't recognize, because it could be a debt collector, a lawyer, a salesperson or the bank trying to take my car, or a friend just calling to say hello; anyway, it made me anxious. I had anxiety whenever I received an invite to any social event. This is especially bad because I am a public speaker. I had a few public speaking opportunities, and I would have anxiety from when I found out about the event, on my way there, during and after the event. I was a mess. There was this joke between myself and my friend, who also doubled as my PR agent, where I would not do any free talk because I was unwilling to get free anxiety. If I were to have anxiety, I wanted to get paid! Thankfully, using the knowledge, principles and techniques I learned and share with you in later chapters, the anxiety is gone, and many other aspects of my life have significantly improved. This has been the case since I received my awakening and started to practise the steps I have included in further chapters.

Ignorance or knowledge? We all have a choice. The biggest mistake a lot of people tend to make, is to think that they know everything. People who think they know everything will not grow. It is that simple. When we think we know everything and live a life of ignorance, we stray away from clarity. We think and act in ways that naturally turn our emotions into worry and doubt, which fills our minds with all kinds of crap that ultimately turns into fear. Fear, my friend, can be a great motivator, however, fear-based decisions and motives are temporary and will only lead to anxiety in the long run. This fear, in our ignorance, fills our being and turns into anxiety, and when anxiety is suppressed in our ignorant state, we become stressed. After some time of not seeing a way out of this pit of negative emotions, we got ourselves into, because we are not conscious that we did this to ourselves in the first place. There is no clarity in ignorance. We only become depressed. We all have a choice, yet not everyone is consciously aware of these choices. This book is filled with knowledge. Ignorance or knowledge? What will you choose?

I chose knowledge, and since then, I have become happier. My businesses have sprouted new feet, learned to walk, and are now jogging again. I have fewer friends, but my friendship bonds are deeper than ever before. I do not party or drink because it just isn't for me. I no longer binge-watch mindless shows as often as I used to, because I have discovered and risen to my purpose and things I am passionate about. I am stress-free, and my anxiety levels are at an all-time low. Not even Coronavirus can mess with me because I have become unfuckwithable. Unfuckwithable is when you are truly at peace and in touch with yourself, and nothing anyone says or does bothers you, and no negativity or drama can touch you. My

FINDING HAPPINESS IN THE FACE OF SUFFERING

confidence is through the roof, I now exercise five to six days a week, and I have regained an eight-pack ab and am getting very good at Calisthenics. My colleagues, business partners and friends, all keep asking me to share with them what I am doing because I am still not rich in the traditional sense, but I am living a rich life. I am still in debt, but I have paid off most of the debts from my financial catastrophe, and I am one of the happiest out of all of us, and they can see it. In this book, I will pass on the knowledge and the mental frontiers I have used to cultivate the happiness I feel. I will pass the ability to you to not only have a direction for where you want your life to go, but to also be in control of your life. If you are experiencing life challenges, which you may or may not, you can also be happy and have a direction to where you want your life to go. Again, I want to emphasize this essential piece of advice: the benefits you get from reading further will depend on your own hunger for self-development and change. The key to every self-help book is to approach its content as if your life depends on it and then very importantly - take action. When you do that, you will discover new and extraordinary possibilities.

What qualifies me to write a book on hacking your growth for happiness? Honestly, anyone can write this book if:

1. they have gone through a massive radical transformation;
2. they have a calling to heal and help others;
3. they can recall the steps;
4. and have backed it up with intensive psychological, scientific, and spiritual research.

ADEWALE ADEJUMO

My name is Adewale Adejumo, I have a Master's degree in plant science, and I have been an entrepreneur for the past 10 years. When I got the awakening of what I described as the next level of my consciousness, I felt an immense urge to help everyone break out of the "sleep" mode in which they are living life. My idea to write this book came about because friends and colleagues who had seen me at my worst and now witness this new version of me, keep asking me what I am doing, and because I keep having to answer the same questions and teach the same things in one-on-one conversations, I have come to identify what a lot of people are doing incorrectly in life regarding their happiness because I was once there.

In addition, growing up in an African home with normalised African behaviours, gave me the motivation to write this book in the hope of changing lives and creating a better way to live our lives. I was born in Nigeria in 1985, my family moved to South Africa in 1997, where I grew up. To make the changes I made, it took me 2 years. In fact, it was 2 years before starting to write this book back in 2018 when I made a decision to stop drinking, but that was not the magic moment when my whole life turned around. Perhaps it was the beginning of my search for a deeper meaning to life, some people call it soul-searching. The reason is that my life did not turn around immediately because I was stressed the entire time:

1. I was unhappy,
2. I tried to smile,
3. I forced smiles,
4. I forced myself to think I was happier, but inside I was depressed, sad, and felt immense suffering from

FINDING HAPPINESS IN THE FACE OF SUFFERING

just being alive.

I was living life like most people who wake up and force themselves to try new things for the sake of it, in an attempt to make themselves happy. I would pick up a new habit without a deep understanding to try and force a more joyful life because I read somewhere that I should try it, or a friend would tell me to try this or try that. I avoided the one thing I needed to do, which was to go deep inside and peel away my ego and stop blaming others. The things that made me unhappy were not the things that happened to me, it was my response to the things that happened. Responsibility is how you respond to situations in your life, and I avoided taking responsibility for my own life. As liberating as it has been to take responsibility for my life, it seemed so daunting back then. For the most part, I didn't even realise that I was creating my own misery, and I did not realise that at any time, I could lift myself out of that misery. It was easier to blame others and not take responsibility. All the while I wanted to be happy, which in and of itself was a paradox. It was the thinking of a fool. A fool is described as someone who tries the same things and expects a different result. That was me.

I did eventually stop drinking. Some benefits of not drinking are saving money, clarity of mind, not finding yourself in messed up situations, , and going out way less. This meant that my mental energy could be used to focus on more long-term goals instead of what the weekend will bring. You will be amazed at how certain things start to come into perspective when you free up your mind from the mind-numbing short-term pleasures of a good time. You start to think longer-term and your actions start to reflect your long-term goals. However, in the state that I was, having free time and living in my own head just meant that I spent an unreasonable amount of time watching Netflix which, well, like I said earlier, added zero value to my life. Netflix is great, don't get me wrong. I enjoy watching a lot of shows, but only as a reward after a productive day or in my allocated rest time and days if I do not have anything else planned.

In chapter 7, I write about techniques for setting long-term goals and actually reaching them. In chapter 8, I write about strategies for setting and achieving your short-term goals, which are techniques I applied to myself, and which millions of other people around the world are also using to achieve results in their lives. They are techniques that helped me with writing this book.

For me to transform myself into the happier version of myself today, I dived into over 70 books in a space of 4 months. When I started to read intensively, my goal was not to be happier, it was to be successful in my work life because I thought having money was all I needed to be happy. I began to read to improve my skills for work and to improve my interpersonal skills and ability to be a better leader. This still did not make me happier. It was only until I truly understood that my happiness would not come from accomplishments. Happiness needed to be a conscious goal. It was when I began to realise that the work required is to be done inside me, that was when I began making changes in my mindset. The first change I made was to take responsibility for my happiness. My happiness was not going to come from making money, a new love, or from my family,

FINDING HAPPINESS IN THE FACE OF SUFFERING

nor was it going to come from friends, promotion from work or from getting a new job. My happiness was going to come from me. Before I scare you away, you do not have to read 70 books in 4 months to become happy. This is why I am writing this book to share the key steps I took to achieving happiness, a stress-free life, a present life I am in control of and a life free of anxiety.

The techniques I am going to share are not techniques I invented. They are techniques I learnt from different experts, that I have applied to my life, and it has made a world of difference. They will open your mind to a whole new way of thinking. However, they will only work if you can accept having a change of mindset and taking responsibility for your own actions. Taking responsibility for your actions involves accepting that you are responsible for every action and decision you have taken in your entire life and it is your actions and decisions that will change your life. Remember that responsibility is your response to any situation that comes into your awareness: any, and all situations.

Your thought patterns have led you to where you are today, and the choices you have made throughout your life were not forced onto you, it was all you; you made those choices. That is the reason why we call it "choice". You always choose. You are where you are today in your life because of *YOU*. Your environment does play a role but the majority of what has led you to where you are today is because of you, your thoughts and your choices. Unless you are a baby and you are reading this, which of course, I know you are not. I will take you through understanding the steps of taking responsibility for the person that you are so that you know that you are solely responsible for where your life is right now.

After you take responsibility, we will move unto the next phase of how you can sharpen the saw. Sharpening the saw is just a fancy way of saying "Work on your damn self". To work on yourself, you need to become proactive with your learning. You need to upgrade your knowledge, you need to upgrade your beliefs because our beliefs are often a product of our environment. Beliefs shape our reality. Imagine if you grew up in another part of the world, or you had different parents, would you have the same beliefs you have today? The same beliefs that have not truly made you happy? Even if your beliefs are based on your culture, our cultures come from our beliefs, and culture in society is not stagnant. It can change under certain conditions, and because times have changed, and the way we live our lives have changed, it is time for our beliefs as a society to also evolve. We create our beliefs from friends, parents, media, teachers, religions, trauma, science, people we look up to etc. Beliefs are great! However, we live in a fast-changing environment, a lot of information just gets passed around, and there is just so much noise. This noise comes with the times that we live in. We live in the age of social media, internet, and global travel. Because of this, our belief systems need fine-tuning, and we need to create these belief systems to guide us and block out the noise. If you want to change your life; change your beliefs. If you're going to transform yourself, strip away your ego.

One of my favourite lines to get you thinking is that "culture is peer pressure from dead people" and without us realising

FINDING HAPPINESS IN THE FACE OF SUFFERING

it, peer pressure can come in many forms. It can come from society, it can come from friends, family, colleagues, social media, TV. Pressure comes from everywhere. And these pressures, without even realising it, have constantly been shaping our thoughts and actions, which have a huge constant effect on our moods, happiness, and actions.

During the steps of working on yourself, you are going to start with the restructuring and the recreation of your own belief system where you learn to live life according to your principles. You will live according to your own beliefs and not according to society, people around you, social media, and pressure from dead people.

I will share with you what aspects of your character you'll need to work on to take control of your life and help you achieve short-term and long-term success. To achieve long-term and short-term success, you must set long-term and short-term goals.

Why should you set long-term goals? Long-term goals give you direction. When you have direction, and you have your "NORTH" of where you want your life to go, everything that you do, everything that you plan to do, will be propelled by your thinking and mindset to take actions in order to accomplish that goal. You will learn how to ensure that you stay on track with your plan every day. You will learn how to create the right habits that put you on track to accomplish your short-term goals so that you can then achieve your long-term goals.

After reading this book, the best way to relearn the lessons and continue to grow, is to teach the techniques to others that are seeking for answers. This is because when you teach something, it also helps with your deeper understanding. This step is part of your contribution. It is not a secret that if you want happiness over a lifetime, you can find it in helping others. For centuries, the greatest thinkers have suggested the same thing: Happiness is found in helping others. You will not only be making yourself happier, but you will also become better if the people surrounding you are better. To some people, the concepts in this book may be common sense, while some will be illuminating. However, what is common sense is not what is commonly practised. This book will help you hack your mind so that you can develop habits that will help you live a healthier, happier and more fulfilling life.

You will not only learn how to hack your own mind for you to start being able to form habits a lot easier. You will also learn the action steps that I took so that you can have a clear map of the key action steps that allowed me to accomplish the drastic changes that I made that took me two years. You will learn those key steps from reading in the next few hours or days. You will stop focusing too much on the past and stop worrying and anticipating the future and simply focus on the present by learning techniques to help you quieten the mind. When you quieten the mind and observe the present, you will see there is so much peace in the now.

Most importantly, I will give you a tool that will take only ten to fifteen minutes of your day. Imagine if you can spend ten minutes doing this every day or every other day and those ten

FINDING HAPPINESS IN THE FACE OF SUFFERING

minutes will make you live a conscious, happier life and allow you to set goals easily while maximising your productivity. Imagine if someone came up to you and said, "Hey, I will take ten to fifteen minutes of your time every day in exchange for twenty-three hours and forty-five minutes of happiness each day". What would your answer be? Would your answer be NO? Wouldn't you say, yes? If you answered yes, then you are ready to move to chapter one. If you answered No, then drop this book right now because it's not for you! I'm kidding, keep reading.

Take Responsibility

For each person on earth, there are two worlds. The world as it comes to be in each moment and the world as we think, hope and fear it is. Of these two, the only true world is the one as it comes to be at each moment - the present. The other world is all in our heads and minds. It doesn't exist. The problem with most people is that they live in their heads and base their present moment on the future or the past instead of being present in the present.

When you let yourself see the world as it is, you can base your actions on reality rather than on the longing and loathing of your heart's desires and mind. When you see the world as it comes to be, you get to experience calmness and bliss.

How can we see the world as it comes to be in each moment rather than as we think, hope, or fear it is? How can we base our actions on reality rather than on the longing and the loathing of our hearts and minds? How can we live a life that is wise and compassionate and in tune with reality? The answer to this is the experience of being awake; where you see the world as it is and as it comes to be so that you can base your response on reality.

The first step to changing your life is by taking responsibility for your reality. Your reality is anything that has come to be in your conscious mind; this includes your thoughts. Your reality is your responsibility because you create your reality from beliefs that determine your way of thinking, which is huge.

What is responsibility? Responsibility is your response and action to every situation that comes into your consciousness. Any situation that you are aware of - how you respond is termed your responsibility. Even if you hear a bird tweeting, your response to the tweeting sound is your responsibility. Whether you choose to ignore it and continue with life - which most people probably would - or choose to look for or at the bird, assuming you cannot see it. Your response to the situation is how you take responsibility for it.

How we respond to situations is often based on our thoughts and interpretations of situations. We carry two types of mindsets that govern how we respond to life situations. They are the victor mindset and the victim mindset. These two mindsets are often affected by past events in our lives and are based on how we see ourselves.

People with a victor mindset live a life that is true to their authentic self while making choices and decisions that help them grow and live happier lives. In contrast, people with a victim mindset seem to blame everyone, themselves, and everything for things that go wrong in their lives with little to no action plan.

Do you have a victor or a victim mindset? A way to tell if you have a victor or a victim mindset is by looking below. If you fall anywhere under Victim Mindset, then you have a victim mindset, and if you fall under the Victor Mindset, then you have a victor mindset.

- Victim Mindset

FINDING HAPPINESS IN THE FACE OF SUFFERING

- Negative thoughts, worry, and what-ifs consume their thinking

- They ask: "Why does everything bad happen to me?"

- Always focus on problems or why something won't work

- "If only I had put more into this relationship, he/she would still be with me."

- Engage with any thought that comes into their mind

- Speak death

- "I have no choice! This isn't my fault!"

- Controlled by fear

- "My bosses are biased against me. They've never appreciated anything I've done for this company."

- Have low self-esteem, self-worth, and self-confidence

- "Because of my parents, I ended up this way."

- Wear masks to protect themselves from being vulnerable.

- They blame God and "everyone."

- Victor Mindset

- Positive thinking, hope, faith, and trust in the Divine consume their thoughts.

- They understand that bad situations do not represent who they are and take it as a necessary part of their growth journey.

- Focus on finding solutions - believing why it will work out

- "This has already happened. What can I do to change from this day onwards?"

- Practice thought control and holding their thoughts captive.

- Speak life

- "I accept these circumstances as part of life."

- Operate out of love

- "I've done my very best, things may not be great right now, but I can choose my own future."

- Know their worth, have healthy self-esteem and self-confidence

- "The challenges I had growing up made me a stronger person. I embrace everything."

FINDING HAPPINESS IN THE FACE OF SUFFERING

- Live as their authentic selves.

- They take responsibility for everything in their life and don't blame God or anyone.

How you respond to every life situation is your choice, and that choice determines the quality of the life you will live. You can gain control over your responses by developing a victor's mindset.

- Victim Mentality

I grew up, and I currently live in South Africa, which is arguably one of the best countries to live in Africa. It has excellent infrastructure, beautiful weather and provides many opportunities for its people to excel and become successful. South Africa, like a lot of countries, is not without its woes. It has high unemployment and crime rates as well. One of the main things I have visibly seen plaguing a large sum of South African people is the victim mentality. This is something I have picked up over the years of living here. I have lived in South Africa for 23 years and I love it. During a conversation I was having with one lady in her 30s about why she was unhappy, I picked up that she was harbouring a victim mentality.

I had asked her about her family life, and she told me that life had been hard for her because she is a middle child, that she blames her mother for her inadequacies and shortcomings in life. She said she was not loved like her other siblings and blamed her mother for her negative emotions.

Here's the thing about most people on this planet; most people need healing from their upbringing. Our parents, just like you and I did the best they could with the knowledge they were equipped with and even now. Holding on to the past and wanting the expression of love we never had will not help you in the present. The best anyone can do for themselves is to focus on their personal growth and healing so that you adopt a different energy to the one you were programmed with from childhood. So that you can become the person you wish you had growing up. If you are always in a state of anxiety, stress, and of a reactive mind — what type of energy are you teaching your kids to adopt? The buck of victimhood has to stop with you.

The thing about a victim mindset is that it is easier to adopt one when you lump yourself with a cause of a group of people. Hence when people see themselves as victims, they use they/ us/ we instead of me/ I and you. In our conversation, I had asked her to try a little exercise by saying "I" and "ME" instead of "WE" and "US".

I listened to her while she told me about the bible and how "they" (white people) have tried to brainwash "us" (black people) by depicting Jesus as white. I will use her words from here on; she said: "I have always had this thing where to them the bible is to try and brainwash us from having a lot of questions, because the more we question things, the more we will discover our purpose and the more knowledge and power we will have within us. They have oppressed our minds because our minds are a weapon. The mind is the biggest weapon, more than a gun, knife, or bomb because the mind does powerful things. That is how I have always felt; like my mind is capable of so many things and it is just a matter of unlocking certain doors or putting puzzles together. Yet again, I say I am Christian, but I start to question this and that part in the bible, and then I find myself questioning the whole book. Then the scary part is that they have made us fear that the moment you start to question all of this, at some point, you are going to grow up, and you are going to question the bible, they will use certain verses in the bible. The truth is that they are trying to make us fear the unknown. Fear the fact that my reason for questioning the bible is that I believe in something else or because I am possessed by evil."

Then I asked her: "who are they?"

She said: "The white people. They stole everything. They said God is a white person. They make us think that the first people who were here were white people and that God is a white person. They said that the sun and the cross came from them meanwhile, the sun and the cross came from the Egyptians". I continued to listen in silence. She then said: "I have the strongest sense that we were fed crap and bull and shit, stuff like that. To believe certain things while it was never like that and they took everything from us, painted this world for us not to question, and because the internet is there, certain things are coming out to us and are making sense as to why things were the way they were and why we are as strong as we are." Then I asked her permission to share something I learned during my process of taking responsibility, which is that a lot of people always say "We" or "You" or "Us" but do not say the word "I". This is because when they say "I", it has a different ring to it.

That ring is "**responsibility**". It exposes how a person responds to a situation, especially when you say out loud. So, I asked her to replace the "We" in her sentences with "I".

Here's what happened; She said, "I strongly believe that they took everything from me". She then stopped and asked, "How did they take everything from me?". That was the point! We complain less when we become responsible. She immediately saw the difference when she used "Me" and "I", and she became more present in her words. This little exercise of saying "I" was a key action moment for me to stop blaming factors out of my control for my misfortunes and for me to start taking responsibility for my life. Blame is the reaction of a wounded ego. Blame gets in the way of our happiness. An essential step to being truly happy is accepting responsibility for everything in your life, which requires putting aside your ego.

It takes courage to take responsibility and own your shit. Fact is, you'll be happier when you take responsibility for everything in your life. The happiest and most successful people in life take responsibility and are accountable for everything in their lives. They do not play the blame game. Have the courage to face your failures, own them, embrace them, and use them to grow.

When you use "I", it doesn't only make it easy to stop complaining, it makes it easier to start taking responsibility and taking control of your life. You get to see how your response to a situation affects your being. It also makes it easy to start appreciating the things you already have.

FINDING HAPPINESS IN THE FACE OF SUFFERING

You are responsible for everything that has happened in your life up until now. Take a look at how you respond. Does your response help you grow, or does it leave you in the same place or worse off? Taking responsibility is a choice. Action or no action is a choice. You are responsible either way as long as anything comes into your awareness - go back to the bird's tweeting example.

Our actions can result in either good or bad things happening. When good things happen due to our contribution, most people do not struggle to say: "Hey, I made that good thing happen" and want to take the praise.

Where most people tend to struggle is accepting accountability when things go wrong. In business, we tend to blame the economy, we blame the past, we blame our staff and our government or president. We look for a scapegoat. A few people will admit they contributed to a poor outcome, however, being responsible means that you must step up and take ownership even for the adverse outcomes. If your choices ever caused something to happen, then you are accountable. If you do not take accountability and respond appropriately, then you cannot truly start with solving the problem. A person with a victor's mindset will own up and take responsibility in a manner that can begin the step towards solving a problem, which is the first step towards growth and taking control of your happiness. Those who do not accept responsibility for their own emotions and actions will repeat the same mistakes and wonder why bad things keep happening to them.

It is part of human nature to cause things to happen. As humans, we are the only animals with the power to consciously choose how we want to shape the world. Our choices - which sometimes are not intentional acts - determine the outcomes in our lives. We may feel bad over certain outcomes. However, being responsible means that you own up regardless of the outcome, and this is not always the easy thing to do. Once the outcome has been revealed, it can be difficult to say that you were the cause of it.

Those people who refrain from being responsible for their outcomes do so because they do not understand the truth behind being responsible. I used to be one of "those people". There are 2 fundamental aspects of being responsible that you must understand; "being responsible is not taking the blame", "being responsible is positive".

Being responsible is not taking the blame because blame insinuates that you did something deliberately. When we are issuing blame, we are usually looking for a scapegoat. We are not really looking for a solution. We just want to avoid responsibility. Being responsible is accepting that a mistake was made, identifying that mistake, and rectifying it. Rather than looking for a scapegoat, you are looking for a way forward.

When you are **responsible, this is about being positive and being solution focused.** It is not a sign of weakness to take responsibility for your mistakes. It is a sign of supreme confidence. You know that you made a mistake, and you are confident enough to know that you can rectify it. Positive beliefs lead to positive actions and better outcomes.

FINDING HAPPINESS IN THE FACE OF SUFFERING

I lived a sad and miserable life until I sat down with myself and started taking responsibility for the things that were happening in my life. Things such as my business going down and my relationship that fell apart. These adverse outcomes were not deliberate. I mean, who wants to fail in their business and relationship life? However, I would have never started to take rectifying steps until I came to terms with my own shortcomings. I saw how my life had been a series of choices which I had no clue what I was doing a lot of the time even when I thought I did. I refreshingly realised that my life was the way it was because of:

1. my actions,
2. my mindset,
3. my lack of knowledge,
4. my inadequate leadership skills,
5. my lack of empathy,
6. my inability to set goals,
7. my inability to truly be a happy person,
8. my inability to stick to a plan,
9. and that I was distracted.

"WHEN YOU TAKE RESPONSIBILITY, YOU CAN GENUINELY CHOOSE WHAT OUTCOME YOU WANT IN YOUR LIFE. THOSE WHO DO NOT WILL LIVE A LIFE DETERMINED BY PAINFUL LESSONS"

Everything that had happened in my life had happened because of me. I took responsibility, and I started to identify all the actions that let me be where I was in life in 2019. My thoughts which translated into action, my values, and my principles were all influenced by the environment I was in, my circles of friends, and the content I consumed. Until I took responsibility and started saying I did this, and I did that, I could not begin to rectify the things that had gone wrong and start shaping a better future for myself. When I took responsibility, I had a clearer mind and gained confidence, which naturally led me to start looking for solutions and led to a positive outcome. Only when I took responsibility did I then begin to make the correct choices necessary to resolve my problems.

I realised that I was living where I did not want to live. I admitted to myself that I chose to live there. It was not because of my business or for love, it was because of me. I was responsible for where I lived. I was responsible for my environment and the people in it. If I am responsible for all these things, then I can change them. I can change my environment. I can change people around me. I can change where I live to better suit how I want my life to look. I can read more. I can love. I can be more present. I can be kinder.

I wrote down acclamations and said them out loud so that I can hear everything I am responsible for, and I can start to act. When I write things down, I get them out of my head, and I can look at them from a new perspective. This helped me a lot, and below are some of those acclamations.

I am responsible for:

- The things I own

- The content I consume

FINDING HAPPINESS IN THE FACE OF SUFFERING

- The people I let into my life
- The way I spend money
- The clothes I buy
- The clothes I wear
- The friends I hang out with
- The parties I go to
- The time I spend on my growth
- The time I spend with my family
- My education
- Working on myself
- My life
- How I react to the way people act towards me
- My wellbeing
- My health
- My mental state
- My reaction to my environment
- Waking up early

ADEWALE ADEJUMO

- Going to be early
- Getting enough sleep
- Sitting still in front of the tv and watching it while the world continues to move forward
- The people I follow on social media
- The people I unfollow on social media
- All my subscriptions
- How much I choose to spend on my car
- How much I choose to pay for my home
- My debts
- The way I treat my colleagues
- The way I pick up a call
- Whether I pick up calls or not
- My response to telemarketers
- My Beliefs
- The way I live my life
- The traditions I follow
- Creating new habits for my life

FINDING HAPPINESS IN THE FACE OF SUFFERING

- Creating own belief systems
- My confidence
- My joy
- Taking a walk
- Resting
- Meditating
- The way you make me feel
- The grudges I carry
- Forgiving
- Exercising
- My Goals
- My plans
- My spirituality
- My generosity
- My positive connections

Because they are all my choices. These are actions that I chose to do or not to do. We are responsible for every choice we make regardless of how conscious we are of the consequences of those choices. Oftentimes, we are our own worst enemy, and our mindset and actions determine the quality of our lives and the level of our happiness. Happy enlightened people are constantly aware of this. The next time something happens that requires you to respond positively or negatively, which response will you choose?

Do you want to take responsibility for everything in your life? Do you want to take the action of taking control of your life? If you answered yes, try the exercise of writing down all the things in your life that have caused any pain or negative emotions and write down what choice you made or/and are pushing to continue to feel this pain. Write down what you know you have to do to make things better and then do it. Taking responsibility for your actions and accountability for the results is taking control of your own life and your happiness.

FINDING HAPPINESS IN THE FACE OF SUFFERING

Live Your Own Principle

Imagine a remote village community that has had little or no contact with the outside world. In this village, the decisions are made by the elders, and knowledge is also passed on from generation to generation. In this community, the people are generally happy. The customs, attitude, and beliefs of the people make up their culture. Under the right circumstances, the culture of the residents can change from situations that arise both from within the village - which are known as internal factors, and at times, the culture of the collective may change due to external factors from the influence of other cultures.

Let's examine how a culture can change internally in this village. A culture change can take place due to philosophical changes, technological advancement or the people might decide to revolt against the decisions of the elders. They might discover that washing your hands (#coronavirus #washyourhands #facemasksaveslives) is better than religious rituals and better at preventing illness. They might discover that farming is better at providing more food for the village than fishing. All of this contributes to cultural changes due to people finding alternative ways of doing things.

External factors that can influence the changes in culture occur through diffusion and trade of ideas between different cultures. This happens when contact occurs between this remote village and the outside world.

Changes in culture often happen because we find better ways of doing things. And sometimes, some changes are so new that although they were created to make our lives better, we, us, humans, find ways to misuse them because we forget the basic principles of what makes us happy, which is gratitude, kindness, forgiveness, self-discipline, purpose, and love. When we forget these basic principles and live based on how the media or rules made by people that died hundreds of years ago and in some cases, thousands of years ago, in the current time, we will be unhappy.

The reason a lot of us are unhappy is that we live our lives based on peer pressure—these pressures come from tradition, culture, social media, TV, friends, or family.

So, if you find yourself questioning your beliefs and culture, then well done, you are human. You are a perfectly normal human being. The reason this is normal is that you are your own unique human with your own unique mind to look for and invent new ways of doing things better.

We now live in a world with the internet and social media, we are a lot more exposed to the rest of the outside world and at some level, more open-minded. How open-minded you are is based on the amount of new factual knowledge you consume and retain. It is no longer a situation where you only grew up in one area, and only see strangers from the other side of the world when they visit your city. We have access to so much more information now, and we are exposed to so much that it would be abnormal not to question what you know. Here's the truth; you only know what you know. You do not know what you don't know. The fact of the matter is that we are all ignorant to a degree. This is because there are billions of people who have lived and died, and 7.7 billion people on earth who know what you don't know. These people are living different lives and experiencing life through their own lenses. So you really don't know much at all, and unless you expose yourself to new information and become proactive with your learning, you will not learn much about life.

> "THE WORLD DOES NOT CARE ABOUT YOUR FEELINGS AND EMOTIONS. THE WORLD REACTS TO YOUR ACTIONS."

Our environment, basically, what we are exposed to, influences our thoughts, and our individual thoughts have the power to shape our reality. That said, so much of the cultural belief systems that we grew up with are outdated, we live in a different time, and this year is so different from the 1500s or the 1970s, or the 1990s. Fun fact: The cultural belief systems that exist were all man-made, and we can make new ones. Look around you. Everything man-made did not exist nor was invented when most of our beliefs were invented. And like everything man-made around you, your beliefs need upgrading, which is your responsibility. No one is going to upgrade it for you.

Living your principle requires making courageous decisions and not making decisions based on fear or what others may think.

Traditions, if they are long-lasting, are demonstrably consistent with survival in ways that alternatives might not be. Secondly, traditions provide consistent reference points or fixed goalposts in people's lives across generations. This helps social cohesiveness, allowing people to speak the same language, enjoy comparable cultural forms, etc. However, as the world changes and evolves, traditions also need to develop through upgrades that are not happening fast enough.

Upgrading your belief system is about creating a new higher standard way of living. Upgrading your beliefs should bring together the best parts of thousands of years of teachings combined with our ability to now measure the effects of these teachings through science.

In the same way we know that eating natural foods is good for us but have not been able to measure just how much until recent times due to scientific advancements. We now know that certain principles taught across the 7 major cultural regions across the world are good for us. What are these teachings?

- They teach us to be curious and keep learning - Mind
- They teach us to live simple lives - Mind
- They teach us to live healthily - Body
- They teach us to be compassionate - Mind
- They teach us to be grateful - Mind
- They teach us to be forgiving - Mind

FINDING HAPPINESS IN THE FACE OF SUFFERING

- They teach us to set long term goals - Aspirations

- They teach us to set short-term goals - Aspirations

- They teach us to be disciplined - Aspirations.

- They teach us to believe in ourselves and God - Spirituality.

How can we have people living differently and living in different modes of reality? And at the end of the day still living happy lives? Their lives are carrying on as we speak. Look, at the very least, what this should inform you is that there is no one mode of reality we should live in. The one thing all these beliefs have in common is that they were all created by humans.

Since you are human and are experiencing life with the knowledge that did not exist thousands of years ago, you can create your own model of reality that works for you with the lessons from some of the best practices from around the world. When I learned this, I realised that I could live my life on my own terms and I am. And since I started to live this way, I have never been less stressed, nor do I feel pressured. I don't feel pressure from dead people, I don't feel pressure from family, I don't feel pressure from society, and I do not feel pressure from friends.

According to Wikipedia, yes, I'm quoting Wikipedia. "Peer pressure is the direct influence on people by peers, or the effect on an individual who gets encouraged to follow their peers by changing their attitudes, values or behaviours to conform to those of the influencing group or individual. This can result in either a positive or a negative effect or both." For any aliens reading this book: Wikipedia is a multilingual online encyclopaedia created and maintained as an open collaboration project by a community of volunteer editors using a wiki-based editing system.

In most cases where we are unhappy, it is because we are living based on pressures from others that do not align with our being.

Here's the truth, there is no one stopping you from learning, and nothing is holding you to your view or your way of thinking. The only person stopping you from changing your way of thinking is you. It does not matter what race or what religious or non-religious beliefs you have; we all have beliefs in something we were raised to think. Your ability to question those beliefs is your humanity shining through. What makes us different from every other animal is the ability to question beliefs.

You can create your own belief systems and your own reality based on your updated knowledge and information. This is because your belief system starts in your mind, and your mind is what you project to the world around you. Therefore, when you travel and experience the different ways and cultures lived by people from different parts of the world, you see that they live differently, yet their lives are normal. What this tells us is that there is NO one way to live. The way a lot of us live that generally makes us unhappy can be easily changed if we want to and if we know how to. The way we live is only principles to live by, but there are no rules to belief systems. I need you to

FINDING HAPPINESS IN THE FACE OF SUFFERING

understand that to make a change in your life and happiness, you require a change of mindset—a paradigm shift. A paradigm shift is defined as a fundamental change in an approach or in underlying assumptions. It is also defined as an essential change that happens when the usual way of thinking about or doing something is replaced by a new and different way. This discovery will bring about a paradigm shift in our understanding of evolution.

The usual way of thinking did not lead me to happiness. The usual way of thinking has not led the majority of humankind to happiness. However, look at different parts of the world. You will find different ways of thinking and some similarities in ways of thinking that are shown to cultivate happiness. These ways of cultivating happiness have been around for thousands of years. They have been mostly snubbed because there was no way of truly measuring happiness. The Buddhist monks have been telling us for years that meditation is the best way to cultivate happiness and now with the help of science, we know that the Buddhist monks were right all this time.

The approach to living a life filled with happiness has been practised by Buddhist monks for thousands of years. Through meditation, monks can cultivate happiness. The keyword here is "cultivate". Happiness is a skill that you can develop. When you are born, you are a clean slate, and you learn and acquire skills as you grow older. A lot of the things that make you unhappy are things that you learned, so you can learn skills to make you happy. We are sent to school and taught things, but no one teaches us the skills to be happy, specifically. The skill to be happy is what we have learned from monks - the happiest people in the world and science backs it up. They do it through meditation.

Meditation is defined as a practice where an individual uses a technique – such as mindfulness, or focusing the mind on a particular object, thought, or activity – to train attention and awareness, and achieve a mentally clear and emotionally calm, and stable state. There are different types of meditation, most of which can seem boring and will cause even the most disciplined person to quit. Tibetan Buddhist monk Matthieu Ricard, a Buddhist monk with over 40 years of meditation experience, who became a confidante of the Dalai Lama, gave a viral TED Talk, and also a bestselling author said meditation is nothing mysterious. That you don't need to be sitting trying to empty your mind with incense around you under the mango tree. A daily meditation practice among Buddhist monks focuses directly on the cultivation of compassion. This involves envisioning negative events and recasting them in a positive light by transforming them through compassion. This type of meditation is known as Visual Meditation.

Visualisation involves creating a picture in your mind, almost like you are watching TV. You can either picture an event from the past or the outcome of something before it's happened, whether that's a task or opportunity at hand. When I was an athlete doing long jump and triple jump, I used visualisation to help me picture the jumping techniques my coach would show me in videos from some of the best long jumpers such as Carl Lewis and Mike Powell. Being able to picture myself doing the moves and techniques sped up my learning of jumping techniques. I used the visualisation techniques before any jump

FINDING HAPPINESS IN THE FACE OF SUFFERING

I was learning at training and before jumps in competition. In athletics, this is called sports visualisation. It is used by many high-performing athletes. In preparation for the Sochi Winter Olympics in 2014, Canadian bobsledder Lyndon Rush credited imagery with helping him keep his head in the game throughout the long, arduous four years of training between the 2010 and 2014 Olympic Games.

Below are some of what some top sportspeople have to say about visualisation:

Rush: "I've tried to keep the track in my mind throughout the year. I'll be in the shower or brushing my teeth. It just takes a minute, so I do the whole thing or sometimes just the corners that are more technical. You try to keep it fresh in your head, so when you do get there, you are not just starting at square one. It's amazing how much you can do in your mind."

Emily Cook, veteran American freestyle skier and three-time Olympian, described how her specific imagery scripts and mental rehearsal involving all the senses have helped her maintain longevity in her sport.

Cook: "Visualization, for me, doesn't take in all the senses. You have to smell it. You have to hear it. You have to feel it, everything."

Cook: "I would say into a [tape] recorder: 'I'm standing on the top of the hill. I can feel the wind on the back of my neck. I can hear the crowd,' kind of going through all those different senses and then actually going through what I wanted to do for the perfect jump. I turn down the in-run. I stand up. I engage my core. I look at the top of the jump. I was going through every little step of how I wanted that jump to turn out."

Nicole Detling, a sports psychologist with the United States Olympic team, explains the importance of having a multi-sensory approach when visualising.

Detling: "The more an athlete can imagine the entire package, the better it's going to be."

Visualisation is a powerful technique to train the brain, and it is one of the best methods of meditation which is easy to learn and practice and is not boring.

Tibetan Buddhist monk Matthieu Ricard suggests that a person starts with Visual Compassion Meditation. This is a type of meditation that requires you to think of someone who makes you happy and focus on your altruistic love for them. Altruism is showing selfless concern for the well-being of others, which is being unselfish. Altruism and love go hand in hand. A person cannot be said to love unconditionally without being altruistic, nor can a person be altruistic without loving unconditionally. Unconditional love is a concept comparable to true love.

"We all have unconditional love for a child or someone dear," he said. Such moments of love usually "last 10, 15 seconds, one minute, then we'd do something else, we go about our work. But suppose you take that beautiful, strong warm feeling, and instead of letting it disappear after 15 seconds, you cultivate it for five, ten minutes, by reviving it. Coming back if you are distracted, keeping the clarity, the vividity, the vividness

FINDING HAPPINESS IN THE FACE OF SUFFERING

of that." This is the basis of practising compassion using visual meditation.

After practising that simple meditation exercise, you can begin to spread that compassionate feeling to other specific people, or strangers around you, or a particular part of the world.

As the many studies Ricard has participated in have proven; the mind reacts to this type of meditation, and the brain actually develops a stronger capability for emotional control.

This is a meditation practice that I and millions of people around the world practice. Before I started practising meditation, I was miserable. I was so miserable that I would try anything and read anything, and that was what made me try meditation. I have since learned many different types of meditation since I started my meditation journey. Did you know that you can meditate while taking a walk and even while driving? You can chant during meditation and sometimes, even just control your breathing to calm down. I will go deeper an effective meditation practice in the chapter on meditation which will transform your days and your being. The compassion aspect of meditation is only 1 of the few steps of the meditation steps you can practice daily.

- Love Yourself: Do Not Put Too Much Pressure on Yourself

The worst criticism we face is the one we make to ourselves, and we should learn to let go of negative thoughts in order to be happy. We should not let our self-criticism kill our vibe. We should not take ourselves too seriously because life will be a lot easier without having self-criticism breathing down our necks. Here are keyways to not put too much pressure on yourself:

1. **Learn to let go** - the best thing you can do for yourself is to let go of the past things that have happened that you cannot change no matter how much you want to. You may have memories from these mishaps to protect yourself from future pains, however, this is also hindering you from your self-acceptance. So instead of carrying these painful memories with you, use them as a learning platform to avoid making the same mistakes in the future. Do not blame yourself. The goal is to take responsibility instead of placing blame because mistakes are just a part of life, and we use mistakes to grow.

2. **Mistakes are okay** - we all make mistakes and sometimes they are unavoidable, we learn from them. Do not hold yourself to an unrealistic standard, do not be afraid to embarrass yourself. If you do not make mistakes, you would not have learned what worked for you. In a really messed up way, mistakes are good because they help us learn, and we should not care too much what others' opinions are.

3. **Stop caring what other people think** - the opinions of others and what they think about you are not important. If you spend your time trying to please everyone, you will just be miserable in the end. We are at our happiest when we live in an authentic way that is true to ourselves and when we care about how we feel and not how others perceive us #unfuckwithable. Once we learn not to put too much value on the feedback from others, be it compliments or criticism, we'll be able to set a standard for our own happiness. At the end of the day, all

FINDING HAPPINESS IN THE FACE OF SUFFERING

that matters is your own happiness and confidence in your own decisions. So, block out what other people say and set your own standard.

4. **You should not stress over outcomes** - the problem with stressing over the outcome is that it stops us from acting in the present because having expectations for the end outcome can be overwhelming and leave us unprepared for the actual outcome. Life is unpredictable so make sure that you are aware that there can be numerous outcomes for any situation, however, when you set a goal for yourself and continue taking the small consistent actions towards your goal, you will often reach your goal or at least get close enough, so keep your mind open, don't let yourself get stuck in a tunnel vision and fall victim to disappointment. The fear of disappointment is what makes us create critical expectations as a way to protect ourselves, but remember that anything can happen, and if you can accept that, you can adapt to that situation.

Look, there's only one you. Be happy about that and stop comparing yourself to others, especially in terms of unrealistic ideals. No one is the same as you or the person you are comparing yourself to. Live your life on your own terms and accept yourself for who you are and for God sake, don't allow yourself to feel inferior because you don't look like someone else. You don't look like an Instagram model and if you do, great for you. Constantly comparing yourself to others forces you to focus on the negative. So be grateful for your unique features, you're the only one who has them, and be grateful for the hand you have been dealt. Focus on what is great about you. Once you learn to love yourself, you'll be able to focus on the positive and let go of negative thoughts that try to creep into your mind. Letting go is probably one of the hardest things to do, but if you can let go of the things that spoil your mood, you'll learn how to focus on the positive things in life and it will leave you free to be happy.

Experience Joy In The Face of Suffering

The only reason you should look back is to see how far you've come. Congratulate yourself and then keep moving forward. I have made mistakes in my life, and I am sure you have too. Actually, I can bet everyone has. Are we the mistakes that we make? Some people will argue yes, some will argue no. I say our mistakes are a part of our biology but we are not entirely our mistakes. Why? Because we learn, change, move on and grow. Each decision we make to hurt ourselves and the people we care about are maybe some mistakes we wish we could go back and change. Because we still hold onto the hope of a perfect outcome, because we refuse to accept what is and let go. Life is not perfect, and neither are we. When we don't accept life's outcomes, let go, and forgive, we hurt ourselves. And hurt people, hurt people.

This is more than a clever phrase. Hurt people hurt other people because they are hurting, and they have been hurt. Each of us has been wounded to one degree or another, and this pain has shaped our views of ourselves and the world in one shape or another. As a result, we often become defensive, protect ourselves at all costs and lash out at others because of our unknowing refusal of how we identify with the situations that we have encountered in the world.

What does that mean? First, we must revisit the definition of what an ego is. Google dictionary defines it as "a person's sense of self-esteem or self-importance." A Psychoanalyst will define the ego as "part of the mind that mediates between the conscious and the unconscious and is responsible for reality testing and a sense of personal identity". In philosophy, it is called "a conscious thinking subject". I call the ego: how you identify with the situations in your world and your mental construct of it. This chapter is going to help you gain an understanding of how to let go of hurt, and how to start conditioning your mind to have better thoughts. You will gain an understanding of the physical changes that occur in your body when you let go, accept and forgive.

Why do we hurt?

We hurt because of our egos. The cause of chronic hurt is normally because we cling to the desired outcome of a situation in the past or future. We cling on instead of accepting and letting go. We do not fully accept our situations in the present. We do not accept ourselves and because of that, we act based on our views of the world which are not based on reality. Still, we want the world to accept us. People who want the world to accept them will always have something to be miserable about forever. Without resolving our hurt by letting go of past issues and letting go of the perfect picture of the situations we want (but cannot have), we will carry our pain with us. The result of carrying around hurt is that we inflict it on others. If you want to have better relationships with others, you first need to have a better relationship with yourself. Our ego has a big part to play in this.

Your ego manifests as the situations in your life you tie your identity to. Identities we created and attached to situations

FINDING HAPPINESS IN THE FACE OF SUFFERING

linked to mental triggers such as our social status, getting a partner and keeping a partner, friendship, and care for loved ones.

These situations are linked to our survival, but it's the wisdom and awareness of these patterns that help us live a more conscious life.

The goal is to realise these patterns because it allows us to change our habits—to control the thoughts that arise and maintain our psychological freedom in their presence.

How to become more aware of these patterns? Please get to know these mental triggers and learn to become aware of them. You can become more aware of them by becoming more mindful. You can become more mindful through mind training practices such as mindfulness meditation. When you meditate, you observe your thoughts as they form during meditation. The more you meditate the more aware you become of your thoughts and the clinging that takes place in your mind. Once you are aware of your thoughts, you can acknowledge or choose to act on them if you wish, but you don't need to be ruled by them.

People tie their identity to their jobs, their looks, the way they dress, speak, some even to the way they walk, their partners, their businesses, their houses, cars, the past they have had and to even the type of future they envision for themselves. That last one - "the future they envision for themselves" is the hardest one of them all. That is the one that causes the biggest pain and suffering for the majority of human beings and what prevents people from simply enjoying the present because their minds get consumed by the perfect ego. We cling to a picture of how we expect things to be because of our ego. The ego where everything in the world and everyone is just as you want it. To me, it is insanity, because the world will never be as you want it. You can change the future, but you must learn to accept yourself in the present and see your life as it comes to be and appreciate who you have become. You need to disengage and stop clinging to how you expect things to be. You need to accept the things you cannot change and make peace with them. After all, you have no control over anything outside of yourself. The only control you have is control over how you react to things in your life. When you start to understand this superpower that you have and note that your reality has been shaped by your attachment to your ego, you can begin to detach yourself from these constructs you have created and start to see the world as it is and accept the world as it comes to be.

Each time you see the world as it is, and bring your mind to the present, you feel blissful, and you live in a beautiful state. That is the power of detachment. Detachment from the past and the future and your mask identity, to become present with yourself.

The ego is the reason we get heartbroken and experience grief. And why it is easier to get over a person dying than a person who broke your heart. Grief is often seen as pain, however it can also be seen as unexpressed love. As painful as grief can be, you can detach easier from an imagined future when the person no longer exists. Your mind is more accepting of things it can see. This is because dealing or getting over grief and

FINDING HAPPINESS IN THE FACE OF SUFFERING

heartbreak are not handled the same way. With grief, you often just need to let go. With heartbreak, you must forgive and let go. This is why it is much easier to deal with grief than it is to get over a broken heart.

When you find yourself in situations where things have not happened favourably for you, and there is nothing you can do to change it, you need to let go of the imagined future you had and forgive the people in the situation. Sometimes, that also means forgiving yourself. I am sure you have heard it time and time again, to forgive yourself. What does it mean? What does it mean to forgive yourself?

Forgiving yourself means to let go of what could have been and accept what is without having negative emotions in the present. So, I'm going to use a very light example here, say you set a target for yourself for meditation and promised yourself you would meditate once a day for 7 days straight, and then on the 3rd day, something happened, or maybe you just did not feel like meditating because you felt tired. Some people feel guilty for not keeping some of the promises they have set for themselves. These promises could vary, ranging from the gym, a diet, studies, to work. If you notice, all these examples are promises to oneself. If you don't keep your promises to yourself, you need to forgive yourself. Forgive yourself for not having created the exact future you had imagined. Forgive yourself and tell yourself you deserve the rest and learn from yourself. Forgive yourself for not doing everything you now know that you could have done to make a situation from the past better. Forgive yourself for hurting the people you love. Forgive yourself for not practicing self-love. Accept that you cannot change the past – love and appreciate the person you have grown into.

Learn from each time you forgive yourself because it has helped to shape you into a better person. I once read a quote somewhere that forgiveness without a behaviour change is just manipulation. This applies when someone asks for forgiveness, receives the forgiveness but doesn't change their behaviour. Why wouldn't this apply to you too? It does. It applies to you. Learn each time you forgive yourself and always look for a better way of keeping your promises to yourself. This takes working on your integrity so that your actions are aligned with your goals and visions. When you start to keep your promises to yourself, you will become unstoppable.

Our ego is essential. It must be used as a tool to help us set targets for ourselves and help us learn, however, it is not who we are. Who we are is what we are in each present moment. It is important to note that you are not your future or your past. Who you are is who you are in each present moment of your life.

I don't want you to confuse your ego with your status. Your Ego is your perceived identity in any situation and personal to you. Your status is how others perceive you to be.

You cannot get rid of your ego, that is simply impossible. Even if you managed to get rid of yours, you'd need to be isolated on Mars to escape other people's egos. Ego is weaved into the fabric of our society, which is why we have social status. It's sad, but it's reality. Social status is a measurement of social value.

FINDING HAPPINESS IN THE FACE OF SUFFERING

Measuring our social value - that's just messed up. And this is tied to your assumed competence, level of honour, and even the level of respect people feel you deserve. Your social status differs based on the company you work for, the colour of your skin, your sexual orientation, the country you are from. Not to even mention the material things society attaches to our social status. So in short, you cannot escape the ego, but you can let go of it and forgive situations and people so that you take control of your ego instead of letting it control you.

Through forgiveness and letting go, you can be able to experience life better. You forgive the past, and you let go of the identity you tie to an imagined future that does not exist. When you forgive the past, you can move on without negative emotions being triggered. When you let go of an imagined future, for example, a future with a person, or a job, or say what you imagined your life would look like in the present. Then you will stop with regrets and be able to make courageous choices in the present.

According to a study titled How the Brain Heals Emotional Wounds: The Functional Neuroanatomy of Forgiveness conducted by Emiliano Ricciardi and several others; it was revealed that forgiveness changes the neuro function of the human brain. It is not just nonsense that people say. It is backed by actual science. In the study, they examined what happens in the brain when you forgive by using functional Magnetic Resonance Imaging (fMRI) to measure the effect of forgiveness on the brain. How is this possible? It is possible because when a brain area is more active it consumes more oxygen and to meet this increased demand, blood flow increases to the active area. This is because a group of neurons sends a burst of electrical pulses to another group of neurons in the brain which creates a wavelike pattern that can also be measured as brain waves. These electrical pulses along with changes in blood oxygen help to create an image that is seen on an fMRI scan.

The study was conducted by giving the participants imaginary social scenarios that described emotionally hurtful events, followed by the indication to either forgive the imagined offenders or harbour a grudge toward them. The participants rated their imaginative skills, levels of anger, frustration, and/or relief when imagining negative events as well as forgiveness. Forgiveness was associated with positive emotional states as compared to unforgiveness. The study showed that granting forgiveness was associated with activations in a brain network, which comprised the precuneus, right inferior parietal regions, and the dorsolateral prefrontal cortex.

This brain network is involved in:

1. **Precuneus**. The precuneus is a brain region involved in a variety of complex functions, 60 of them, which include recollection and memory, integration of information (gestalt) relating to the perception of the environment, cue reactivity, mental imagery strategies, episodic memory retrieval, and affective responses to pain.
2. **Inferior parietal lobule**. This has been involved in the perception of emotions in facial stimuli, and interpretation of sensory information. The Inferior

parietal lobule is concerned with language, mathematical operations, and body image, particularly the supramarginal gyrus and the angular gyrus.
3. **The dorsolateral prefrontal cortex.** The primate dorsolateral prefrontal cortex (DLPFC) has long been implicated in higher cognitive functions, such as switching attention, working memory, maintaining abstract rules, and inhibiting inappropriate responses.

The study found that forgiveness makes us smarter. It makes us more empathetic and improves our cognitive functions. Now, imagine incorporating forgiveness practice in your daily life. The result is a better relationship with people at work, at school, at home, and in public. This is because letting go and forgiveness helps you get rid of negative emotions and feelings. It allows you to be more present so that you can live in a beautiful state and increase the happiness in your life.

Why do we hold on to the source of our hurt, pain, and suffering?

That thing that happened or that opportunity we lost out on, or that person we hurt or lost. It is because we tie our identity to how we want the present and our future to be with the person or that thing or that opportunity. We can end our suffering by detaching ourselves from our source of pain by recognising the source and realising that it is because of our ego. Our ego causes our suffering. Suffering occurs when we attach ourselves to our imagined life in the present. It is madness, yet we do it. Let go of the source of your pain, become aware of it, and detach yourself from it by accepting it because it is. Accept the truth, for the truth is all there is; accepting the truth is accepting reality. When we accept reality, through forgiveness and gratitude practice, this lets us live happily and still pursue our goals fearlessly.

The awareness of the ego silences it and brings us to the present. A technique I use to quickly get my mind to the present is by asking myself: "what am I thinking right now?" then I pause to observe my thoughts. Try it. Ask yourself: "what am I thinking right now?" and try to watch your thoughts. Most of the time, your mind will go quiet when you try to observe it. You can observe your thoughts when you have mastered being an observer, because in most cases, for most people, the mind stops when we become aware of it. Ask yourself again. Ask yourself: "what am I thinking right now?" then quietly observe. See again? In most cases, the mind just goes quiet.

However, that's just a way to quieten the mind. A way to stop your ego from controlling you is by the following principles to deal with what's happening outside of you. The basic principles to live by are to not let your ego control you are:

- Be kind to everyone.

- Forgive everyone quickly.

- Give everyone love.

If you are wondering how to deal with the voices in your head, try the following as well:

FINDING HAPPINESS IN THE FACE OF SUFFERING

- Be kind to yourself.
- Forgive yourself quickly.
- Give yourself love.

Apply those principles to yourself, and you will see your life transform. Loving yourself, forgiving yourself, and being kind to yourself is a process. However, when you go through the process and perform it daily, you will appreciate yourself and realise your worth.

In 2012, I met the woman I thought I was going to marry. She was beautiful, tall, and smart. She made me feel better about myself. Being with her inflated my ego, it made me feel important, and my inflated ego made me feel like I was better than most people because I got the girl. I was living out my dream as an entrepreneur, my business was doing well and growing month over month and year over year. I was head over heels in love with her and my business. In 2016, she left me out of the blue. As if this was not bad enough, my business started to show cracks because I had begun employing more people and I frankly didn't know what I was doing then although my ego was so inflated that I thought I did.

The reason I am telling you this story is that the combination of that heartbreak and business falling apart broke me as an individual because a huge part of who I identified as was tied to the relationship I no longer had, the formerly thriving business which was now falling apart, and I was amassing massive debt. At that time, I did not understand the real meaning of taking responsibility, nor did I fully grasp the concept of shedding your own ego. To be honest, the ego I had assumed was based on the ego I thought looked good for everyone else, which itself is a problem because a lot of people take on the ego they believe makes them look cool to others - A form of peer and social pressure. They put on a mask without an awareness that they are wearing masks. They live a life they think they should live because others love and approve of it instead of living a life that is true to themselves. How do you even know the life that is true to you if you don't know that you are wearing a mask?

We all go through life wearing masks. As a baby, all you did was eat, cry, poop and sleep. Then you started growing up and began to learn masks upon masks and resulted in what you now call adulthood. However, under the mask, you are still just a child, not truly knowing who you are but ready to begin a new life at any time.

It is your duty to do your own internal work to find your real self and walk your path, and one of the steps of that path is knowing your real self. There is no skipping this step if you are to become a happier version of yourself.

I carried what felt like a shard of my former self for three years and struggled to let go of the future I had planned from 2012 up until 2016. Things had changed, I was no longer in this beautiful relationship I wanted for my future, and my business was not doing so well. I was hurting, and I hurt the people around me. I hurt any girl I met and the people I was working with. I longed to get back the person that left me and in so doing, caused myself more pain, hurt, and suffering. All my attempts to build this perfect future I held onto so loathingly

FINDING HAPPINESS IN THE FACE OF SUFFERING

only caused more pain, and I was caught in this cycle for up to three years. I would tell myself that I just need to do this one thing, then this one last thing, and then that one last thing. Until it was three years and all I did was cause myself suffering and hurt others.

It wasn't until I came to the realisation that all my pain and hurt were linked to my choices and my sense of purpose that I began to heal myself. We can either react to a situation or respond to it. The whole time, I had been reacting instead of responding. My ego was wounded. Instead of taking accountability and responding in a manner that would help me get past the hurt and pain, I reacted. When you respond instead of reacting, you take responsibility. The first step I took towards my healing was taking full responsibility for my hurt and my pain because I had created them by refusing to let go of a situation over which I had no control.

The only two things we have real control over are our minds and our actions. There are other actions that I could have taken to help me recover faster from my heartbreak. Firstly, I could have set a clear purpose for my life and not tie it to another human being. Secondly, I could not have tied my purpose to my business either. I feel like this is a great time to tell you to never tie your purpose to anyone, a job, or a company. Your purpose should be tied to you and your contribution to others. This is because anything outside yourself can be taken from you, but no one can take away your service to others. It's yours.

After taking full responsibility for all my choices that created my suffering, I needed to practice letting go and forgiveness.

Forgiveness is said to be when you can remember a situation, a person, or a thing that caused you pain and hurt, and can no longer feel pain and hurt. For you to forgive, you need to feel your hurt. You need to go through your hurt instead of avoiding facing it. Why go through it? If you avoid admitting how much hurt you felt and are still feeling, you will continue to hurt. Hence, it is important to let yourself feel and immerse yourself in the hurt and pain you feel.

To consciously and deliberately feel my hurt, I would meditate for 15 to 20 minutes a day. The purpose of this meditation was to forgive and let go. I would visualise the situations and people that caused me the deepest pain. Try this by imagining and seeing yourself experiencing that most anus act that someone did to cause you pain that you are holding on to. Visualise that situation that makes you wake up from bed sweating and crying. Feel it, go through it, and then let go by feeling any negative emotions leave your body while slowly breathing out. You cannot control what happens to you in life but you can control how you respond to what happens to you.

Live In A State Of Abundance

Oprah, Deepak Chopra, Will Smith, Dwayne Johnson, and some of the world's most successful people have repeatedly said that gratitude was the key to their happiness. This is because both 'abundance' and 'lack' appear simultaneously in our lives. It doesn't matter who you are or how much you have; if you do not have a gratitude mentality or practice gratitude in your life, you will tend to focus more on the things you lack in your life rather than focus on the abundance that's already there. What matters for you is what you choose to focus on. Do you focus on what you have or what you don't have?

Gratitude practice helps you focus on abundance. The thing about life is, you see more of what you focus on. It's like the Instagram and YouTube algorithms, which show you more of the content that you engage with; the same thing happens to us in life. What you focus on is what grows, so if you focus on lack, you will experience more lacking in your life, which is life's self-fulfilling prophecy that is created by your thoughts and mind. If you focus on the abundance you have in your life; you will be more tuned to see opportunities and abundance even when others cannot see them. If you focus on positive things, you will see more positive things happening in your life. If you focus on negative things, you will see more negative things happening in your life.

What is gratitude? Gratitude is our readiness to show appreciation. This quality of being thankful affects our biology by boosting the neurotransmitter serotonin and activates the brainstem to produce dopamine. Dopamine is a chemical that's found naturally in the human body. It is a neurotransmitter, meaning it sends signals from the body to the brain. Dopamine plays a part in controlling the movements a person makes, as well as their emotional responses. The right balance of dopamine is vital for both physical and mental wellbeing. Gratitude research shows that although it might be hard to believe; we literally cannot function without the courteous of goodwill. That is a powerful thought.

Imagine if you could take five minutes out of your day, in the morning when you wake up, to reflect and give thanks for three things that you are grateful for in your personal life and three things you are grateful for in your work life and three things you are grateful for about yourself. In this moment of gratitude, you also visualise a positive vision you have for your life in the next 3 years. Then picture yourself winning an award for this vision you have, with people cheering for you as you receive a trophy because you achieved what you set out to achieve. By doing this 5-minute exercise daily, it results in a complete change in your life for the better. You start to feel optimistic about life - like you are high on happy drugs while being filled with energy to go after your goals.

Well, I did, and the result of this very easy-to-do exercise changed me, literally speaking. I felt like I was high on blissfulness and peacefulness from the second week and for the first three months of gratitude practice every morning and picturing a 3-year goal during my meditation practice when I woke up in the mornings 5 to 6 days a week. This was from December 2019 till February 2020. February 2020 was when I

FINDING HAPPINESS IN THE FACE OF SUFFERING

decided I would write this book and then I started. I have not stopped my gratitude practice, nor have I stopped visualising my 3-year goals. Research shows that having a positive outlook of the future improves your thoughts, which increases your state of happiness. Gratitude practice and seeing prosperity in your life can be addictive, which is why you hardly ever see someone with gratitude practice, and that's a visionary who has stopped being grateful.

Gratitude is addictive. Not in the customary sense that one would associate with that word, however, because acts of kindness and feelings of gratitude flood our brains with the dopamine chemical, which is addictive, because we tend to want to feel it more. We tend to be more kind and give more thanks. When we are truly grateful for something or someone, our brain rewards us by giving us that natural high, and because the feeling is so good, we are motivated to feel it again and become more inclined to give thanks and to do good for others. It's our positive thoughts that make us happy.

Happiness is inside every single one of us, which is why when you want to tap into your happiness reserve, you can do it by going inside yourself. You don't always need it to come from the outside. Sure, money can bring us joy and pleasure, and having a constant flow of money in our lives can help to keep our happiness from dipping below a certain point. However, what happens when you don't have money? What happens when you have lost your job, your business, or your source of income? My rule in life is that if you are still alive, you have something in life to be grateful for. That said, everyone has something inside them to be grateful for, and if you are alive, then you can cultivate your happiness from within. What is cultivation? Cultivation refers to being able to develop or acquire. The fastest way to acquire happiness or to cultivate it is through gratitude practice for the things that are going right.

Gratitude practice is not just about practising gratitude when you close your eyes; it is about making it your way of life. Say thank you to people in the moment of their action towards you because it shows that you appreciate them. When you appreciate people, they will be more inclined to be kinder to you and others.

Passing on acts of kindness can go a long way. Kindness is not something you give then expect to get it back from where it's given. When you give kindness, leave room for the possibility that your act of kindness might not come back to you from the same place. However, that act of kindness you showed to another is often passed on to another person, then that person passes it to another person. That's where the phrase 'pass it on' comes from. Kindness is an act that's passed on long after you have passed it on to another person.

A friend of mine from South Africa learned this lesson at the age of 31 when he ended up homeless in the United States of America with his wife. He had sold his wife a dream and convinced her to leave her job in South Africa as he was planning to do the same for himself. Yeah, he really sold her a dream that entailed going to the USA to study and later return to their home country to either get the jobs of their dreams or stay in the US.

FINDING HAPPINESS IN THE FACE OF SUFFERING

Things were going well because he had gotten them both scholarships and moved to the USA until things stopped going well. So, what happened? Their scholarship payment started coming late - three to four months late in fact. Soon after, they ran out of money, which inevitably resulted in them getting evicted from their home in the USA.

To make matters worse, his wife was on crutches because she had broken her ankle that week. So here they were, homeless, with just six dollars in his pocket. On the night they were kicked out, he was distraught and tried all possible avenues he knew to find out where they could sleep. When I say all possible avenues, I mean all possible avenues. He even went to the homeless guys and asked them where they sleep, and they mentioned a shelter that cost more than he could afford.

All the while, he had left his wife at a café and bought her a one-dollar bottle of water from his remaining 6 dollars. Then he remembered that cheques were still widely used in America, so he decided to look for an apartment close by and fortunately found one. He wrote the landlord lady a $2000 cheque and prayed she wouldn't try to cash it in before any money came into the account, however, this apartment was not going to be ready for another two days. And he had nowhere to sleep that night, no one to go to because this was not his country, so no family or close friends were nearby. This lady could see the pain in his eyes and asked him where he and his wife were sleeping that night, with tears streaming down his face, he told her he had no idea where they would be sleeping. She then told him she had a spare room in her apartment and offered it to him and his wife for the next two days as her guests. This was one of the first acts of kindness that forever changed his life. Relieved and in tears, he thanked her and assured her that the cheque would be fine, he explained that they were expecting payments, albeit were delayed. This woman he met that night understood and let them stay; I should add that the payment did come days later.

While there was a sense of relief, it was accompanied by dread because he still had six heavy loads of bags containing all of their belongings waiting for him to carry, all by himself, due to his wife's broken leg. The first bag took him an hour to drag and carry, to make matters worse, the wheels on the bag broke.

Amid his ordeal, a total stranger driving by stopped to ask if he needed any help, grateful for the offer, he accepted the help. Where he would have needed to do more trips to their new, temporary home, the stranger helped him transport the remainder of the loads with just two trips. This was his personal lesson in kindness, and for the next two days, he learned another lesson in humility and demonstrated it by being as helpful as possible to the landlord. He expressed his gratitude by helping with household chores because he couldn't be more thankful.

Today, he is one of the kindest and most empathetic humans I've ever met because he remembers when others were kind to him when he needed it the most. The lesson here is to remember that kindness is passed on, so don't expect it from the same place you put it but know that your acts of kindness stay with people and that it makes them better humans, which

FINDING HAPPINESS IN THE FACE OF SUFFERING

is ultimately for the betterment of all humanity. That's it. Be kind.

Now back to gratitude...

Research has linked gratitude to increased job satisfaction. When people feel appreciated, and they show appreciation for what they have, they're more likely to be happy with their jobs and more likely to give their hearts in whatever they do. When you say 'thank you' to your colleagues, it increases their job satisfaction. The book: How to Win Friends and Influence People by Dale Carnegie, talks about the best way to make friends and influence people is to make them feel important and special, and one of those ways is to be appreciative and express that appreciation to them.

If you have kids, teach them to say "thank you" because it is good for their health. Research shows that youngsters who took part in daily gratitude exercises reported higher levels of alertness, enthusiasm, determination, attentiveness, and energy.

Toddlers should be taught as soon as they can say their first few words to say, 'thank you'. However, saying 'thanks' shouldn't just be an automatic response. It is important to teach children as soon as they can, to understand the emotion behind the 'thank you' sentiment. Children must understand that part of being happy is to express the gratitude that we all have inside of us freely and eloquently.

Other research has also shown that more grateful people have better heart health and more disease-fighting cells in their bodies.

One of the causes of breakups and divorce is that the people within the relationships do not feel appreciated. Of course, relationships are not that simple, but showing appreciation can act as an effective buffer to divorce and demonstrate how committed partners feel in their relationship. Research by the University of Georgia showed that feelings of gratitude could also counteract the impact of conflict and negative encounters in romantic relationships. When you show your partner and the people in your life that you appreciate them, you will improve your relationships with them. Expressing gratitude freely helps us smile more.

Smiling has surprising health and mental benefits. When you smile, you can hardly have negative thoughts, try it right now; put a huge smile on your face and try to think negatively. If you can have a negative thought, at least I made you smile. Smiling boosts our mood, which helps our bodies release cortisol and endorphins that provide numerous health benefits, including:

- Reduced blood pressure.
- Increased endurance.
- Reduced pain.
- Reduced stress.
- Strengthened immune system.

FINDING HAPPINESS IN THE FACE OF SUFFERING

What are the action steps you can take to add gratitude practice to your life? Write down three things you are grateful for every day, then close your eyes and remember the good feelings you felt and how they happened. When you feel those positive emotions associated with those good things you are thankful for, your mood will be uplifted, and it will be harder to forget those things. We are more inclined to store and remember information that triggers emotions in us - positive or negative emotions, which is why we need to train our minds to focus on the positive ones. Use negative emotions to learn about yourself and others and then learn to let go of them.

Is everything going great for you right now in your life? If you answered no, then now is the best time to be grateful. The best time to be grateful is when things are not going well. Gratitude helps us avoid going down the rabbit hole of negative emotions, which often results in anger, sadness, depression, stress, and anxiety. Then ultimately leading to the victim mindset, and trust me, you don't want to go there. You don't need to have big things to be grateful for. You already have something to be thankful for. Be grateful for yourself. Your life. Your uniqueness.

When I started being grateful for my uniqueness, I started being grateful for the uniqueness in others too. When you appreciate yourself, you start to become more appreciative of others as well. Your level of awareness will increase, not just towards you but others as well. You have to love yourself fully before you can truly love others. The same goes for appreciation. You have to appreciate yourself before you can appreciate others fully.

When everything is going great, and we stop being grateful because we start to feel bulletproof, that's when we start to feel like we are not in control of our lives when things go wrong. Whereas, when you are always grateful, you will hardly feel like you have no control over your life - even when things are going wrong and out of control because you will always have things to be grateful for.

What are the things that keep us from being grateful? The things that keep us from being grateful are gratitude murderers, and I call them as such - murderers. This is because gratitude murderers steal our joy, our health, our relationships, and our success. These self-defeating gratitude murderers are habits we create.

- It is hard to be grateful with a victim mentality.

- It is hard to be grateful when you are envious of what others have.

- It is hard to be grateful when you complain a lot.

- It is hard to be grateful with a scarcity mindset.

These self-defeating habits focus your thoughts on your suffering. Precisely what you are lacking. Try flipping your perspective and concentrate on something that matters to you, that you do enjoy, and that you do 'get.' Shift your attention from what you're missing to what you possess. Please don't waste time blaming or getting angry at those who don't want the same things you do, don't wait for them to come on board or help you get what you want. Leave others out and get busy

FINDING HAPPINESS IN THE FACE OF SUFFERING

taking care of what's important to you. Do what you need to do to make things happen for yourself. And when good things happen to other people, be happy for them because displaying genuine happiness for others can only bring some of that happiness in your soul and life as well. Understand that there is an abundance of good out there and it will keep happening to everyone including you. You would want others to be happy for you when good happens in your life, so why do you not give the same energy to others when good happens in theirs? Wanting someone else's life will only bring you pain because you have yours and you have things in your life to be grateful for.

If you have running water, a bed to sleep in, clothes, electricity, toilets, then you have more than millions of people already. An estimated 16% of the world's population does not have electricity. That's 1.2 billion people. Furthermore, according to CDC.org, an estimated 790 million people do not have access to running water, and 1.8 billion people do not have access to proper toilets.

Gratitude helps you to see what you have and helps you to be a more optimistic person. Here are some ways in which I benefited from gratitude practice, how it has changed my life, and how it made 2020 the best year I've ever had.

- Gratitude helped me to focus on the things I have, instead of on the things that I don't have.

- Gratitude helped me to be more generous and kinder.

- Gratitude helped to see my self-worth, which helped my self-esteem.

- Gratitude helped me be healthier. I used to suffer from anxiety and depression.

- Gratitude helped me feel better about my life because it helped me see that I have a lot going for myself.

- Gratitude helped to improve my relationship with my friends and family.

- Gratitude increased my productivity and helped me reach more goals.

- Gratitude helped me to see the best in others and appreciate everyone's uniqueness.

- Gratitude helped me live in a beautiful state.

In all the benefits of gratitude, which benefits are you strong in, and in which benefit areas do you want to improve on? Write it down to keep a record of the benefits for yourself. When you write these things down, and you come back to them after practicing gratitude for a while, seeing how much progress you have made will motivate you to continue to live in a state of gratitude.

To live in a state of gratitude, you must be careful about the type of media you consume. Gratitude cannot thrive when there is negativity. Most of the news on TV and social media is

FINDING HAPPINESS IN THE FACE OF SUFFERING

negative - avoid it. Curate the content you consume. Unfollow the accounts that only spread negativity and follow accounts that produce inspiring and positive content. When we consume negative media, we can get engulfed in anger, fear, and sadness. Gratitude cannot exist alongside anger, fear, and sadness. With that said, you may not be able to avoid negative people, at least not all the time, so here's a way I handle negative people: by simply understanding that we are all operating under a different level of consciousness and therefore, each person is operating at the level at which they are. With this simple understanding, you can simply accept people for who they are and not let their negativity get to you or engage in their negativity. Finally, my mother always told me as a child to avoid listening to and engaging in gossip.

People that gossip cannot be trusted, and when you gossip, you're telling people that you are not a person to be trusted. Gossip drags relationships through the mud, soils them, and lowers the strength of relationships. Most people recognise that while you are gossiping about someone else today, it could be that you are doing the same about them tomorrow. Gossipers focus on lack.

Both 'abundance' and 'lack' appear simultaneously in our lives. What matters is what you choose to focus on. Gratitude practice helps you focus on abundance. You see in your life and get more of what you focus on and those are the things you are thankful for. Thankfulness reduces the feeling of self-centeredness, greed, anger, resentment, and sadness.

- Improve Your Relationship with Money

The awareness of the energy in which money is received and given is something I learned which boosted my level of happiness. Money is a source of both happiness and unhappiness for most people because we see money as either lacking it or having an abundance of it.

How is your relationship with money? Are you happy when you receive money? I bet you are. How about when you spend money? Are you happy when that money leaves your bank account, hand, pocket? Having a good relationship with money is not about how much money you make or have; it is the energy in which your money is given and received that determines the nature of your relationship with money. The energy in which money is received and given is the flow of money. Money is always flowing in and out of our hands. Most of us are grateful when it is received but are unhappy when given to someone else.

When you think about it, someone else is giving you the same money you are grateful for. Wouldn't you want that person to be happy for you? Then why are we not happy for others when we give them money? If you are giving away money for a charitable cause, there is often a deep feeling of contentment which we can be grateful for. We can be grateful for the ability to help others less fortunate than we are. When you give money for goods or services, you are exchanging value, and you can be grateful for the value you are paying for, as well as bringing joy to others.

The plus side to being grateful and appreciative of giving money is that you start to evaluate the value you are paying for,

FINDING HAPPINESS IN THE FACE OF SUFFERING

and you start to have a better relationship with your money because you will be more conscious of the value of the exchange. Being mindful of the value you are paying for will not only make you more careful of what you spend on, but it will also ensure that you spend on the things that add value to your life, which will increase your quality of life. People that spend on value, gain value. By being grateful and paying attention to the value you are exchanging, you will open your consciousness to more ways to make your money work for you.

Imagine a world where you are grateful for receiving money, and you are also appreciative of giving and spending money. Everyone would be grateful. This is the concept of happy money, in which you are grateful regardless of the flow of your money.

For a huge part of my life, I had focused too much on the lacking part of money. Even when I had an abundance of it to spend, I would spend with a scarcity mindset which unsurprisingly has resulted in a lot of unhappy periods in my life. Spending with a scarcity mindset negatively affected my relationship with my money and those around me.

Now, I'm not saying that you should go and start spending vicariously and squander all your earnings, but if you decide that's what you are going to do, which is your choice, you should give with gratitude and visualise the joy you have passed to the person that's receiving.

The concept of giving money with gratitude was a concept that took me a while to understand. Even after I started to practice gratitude, I still felt negative energy whenever I had to spend money, although I had an abundance of it. It was even worse when I was working on a tight budget. However, even on the tightest of budgets, even if it is your last cent, when you spend it or give it away, be grateful for being able to pass that flow of energy to the person you are helping.

When I finally learned of happy money, I started to say 'thank you' every time I would spend money. Whether in person or online. I would say 'thank you' when I would receive an SMS notification of a subscription - Those SMSs a lot of us love to hate, and that filled us with dread were turned into a positive life experience because (1) I was blessed to afford this opportunity to spend. (2) My spending was energy I passed to someone, which brought positivity to the life of the receiver.

Are you ever upset for saying something kind? Do you ever feel dreadful for doing something that makes someone else's life better, especially when it is an exchange? If your answer is yes, then you may need to look at whether you are true to yourself, and it might be time to set boundaries. However, most people would say 'No'. So, why do we sometimes dread spending? It is because we focus on scarcity, whereas money is abundant. There's money everywhere, and it's in constant flow. Money will always flow in and out of your life. The more grateful you are for the flow of your money, the more 'happy money' you will have in your life.

If you base your decision on what you lack and fear, then you will experience unhappy money. To receive happy money, you must shift your mindset to one of gratitude and joy.

Owning Less Means Having More

Imagine you are on holiday for a week and all you have with you is your bag with clothes for the seven days you will be on holiday. Let's throw in your laptop and your phone because you might want to check some emails or send or receive messages on your phone to stay in touch with your loved ones or take pictures to post on social media. Now, let's imagine you are staying in a five-star hotel. In your hotel room, you have your big, beautiful king-size bed, with a couch, TV, desk and chair, a Nespresso coffee machine, a classy painting on the wall, and an elegant bath shower and toilet. Wait! You also have clean towels; actually, everything in the room is clean. Of course, you have the hotel's complimentary sewing kit, soaps, shampoos, toothbrushes, and toothpaste. Breakfast and dinner have been included in your hotel stay, so in the morning, you'll go down to the hotel restaurant and have a buffet breakfast. In the afternoon, you're out and about, maybe sightseeing or having meetings; I never said it was a non-work holiday. So, in the afternoon, you might have lunch somewhere and then in the evening, you have a supper buffet style again at the hotel. Did I mention that the food is absolutely amazing? Imagine this being life for seven days. Away from it all! Awesome right? Well, that's what having a minimalist experience is about. A minimalist experience is a life that feels like you are on a vacation that you will not need to get away from.

I got to experience this imaginary life in May 2019 while trying to figure out what to do with my life. I was living in Pietermaritzburg, South Africa at the time, and my business of

8 years was not doing well, which meant I had to cut down on business costs and the rent was a cost I felt we did not need. I mean; why do you need to pay for rent if you are a tech business? If everyone works off a laptop, you surely do not need a fancy elegant office, which was what we had. I would not want a cheap regular rundown office because I believe that everyone should be roaring and excited to go and be at work because the environment is beautiful and blissful. A beautiful environment definitely contributes to the joy of going to the office. Anyway, I had just closed down our offices, and all the employees were asked to work remotely. Due to this, we could all pretty much work from and live anywhere we wanted. I wanted to move to another country. I had shortlisted Cape Town, Malaysia, Thailand, and Indonesia. Yes, I know, Cape Town is not another country! But it was on my shortlist because, in 2012, I had planned to move there, so I had to find out for myself if I still wanted to move to the aforementioned city, so, in March 2019, I took a trip to Cape Town, and I discovered that it wasn't for me at the time. Cape Town is a beautiful city, but an important aspect of what makes a place pleasant to live, for me, is the weather. In Pietermaritzburg, I had experienced probably one of the most schizophrenic weathers in my life, and I wanted a bit of predictability when I left my home in the morning. I didn't want summer in the morning, winter at noon, hailstorm in the afternoon, then a hurricane for dessert. Or winter when I'm in the shade and summer in the sunlight. So Cape Town wasn't for me at that time. I won't completely say no to living there in the future, because things change. Who knows what the future may bring?

FINDING HAPPINESS IN THE FACE OF SUFFERING

In May 2019, I had a meeting in Durban and was booked into the Hilton hotel for 2 nights by a friend, and all I had with me were my laptop and clothes for two days. In the hotel room, there was a bed, table to do work on, a tv, shower, coffee machine, and couch to relax. My stay at the hotel came with breakfast and supper. So, in the mornings, I'd go down to the hotel restaurant for breakfast and make sure I take some food with me back to my room to save money. I mean; I was on a tight budget! So I'd pack pastries to sustain me for the day. Had my meetings during the day, and then, in the evenings, I'd go down again for supper.

Being in a hotel environment at that stage in my life was a well-needed break that caused a breakthrough for me. I realised one thing, and it was that - that hotel setup was all I really needed. A place with a bed to sleep on. A desk to work on. A couch to sit and relax, a shower, and food.

What followed after that was a search for a beautiful studio apartment that provided those basics. I was intentional about the condo being beautiful and in a location which felt like I was on vacation because as people, we need certain beautiful things in our lives. As humans, we like beautiful things. Every one of us likes beautiful things, and not just in terms of the human exterior. But even in pieces of artwork, furniture, our houses, and the environments around us. These all affect us in subtle, but relatively profound ways.

Beauty from an evolutionary standpoint implies strong reproductive capabilities, which allows us to attract more successful mates.

Beautiful objects like artwork, furniture, our houses, and the environments around us whisper to us the important truths about the good life. Beautiful objects have a special significance for humans because they can be therapeutic, bring a sense of excitement, harmony, peace, and can help free our minds of clutter.

Beautiful things do make us happy unless that beautiful thing takes away your peace and time. A beautiful home or a beautiful car or delicate items are great to have. Still, it's when maintaining that beautiful something becomes a job and consumes our time from other important things in our lives that it is sometimes not needed.

If you have ever been on a holiday or a vacation, you don't have to imagine it, you can remember it. You can remember the feeling of being away from it all. You can remember just how peaceful it is to have just what you need, and you can entirely focus your time on yourself and what you want. Holidays which you book into a nice hotel or condos are nice because you get to experience a minimalist life. Ever thought of it that way? And don't get me wrong, I am not saying to leave your home and get yourself a studio apartment although I did just that. For me, it worked because I am a bachelor with no kids. You have to find your idea of what minimalism means to you.

Most of us remember our stuff-free life when we go on vacation, or remember when you were just a student and you stayed in a commune or student residence? Ok, maybe student life is not a very good example. Let's take the case of a dream lounge, kitchen, or bedroom you see on Pinterest or a

FINDING HAPPINESS IN THE FACE OF SUFFERING

showroom of a retailer. Do you remember how beautiful and desirable they were? They are so clean and only have what you need. THAT is a kitchen, lounge, or bedroom you want to come home to every day. The type of sanitary environment that has what you need and does not have what you do not need.

The jolt we get from the everyday routine that we get from a vacation can help us put our stuff into perspective into what is really needed in our lives. In the grand scheme of things, our material possessions are not that important, and we can weaken the power they have on us if we're willing to let them go. I know some people might be thinking that there is joy in buying new things. I can assure you that there is indeed a joy in that, however, that joy is momentary and quickly dissolves as soon as you have acquired that something you want. There is also joy in letting go of your possessions which lasts much longer. There is joy when you give away clothes you do not wear, sell gadgets you've never used, give away shoes you have never worn, or throw away things that are just not nice anymore. The joy of letting go is a much more lasting one that fills us with peace and serenity.

I have a car that I do not drive much. I would be paying about three-tenths of my car fees if I Ubered and rented cars when I needed to take long drives, which is hardly ever. Imagine, I could eliminate car repairs, monthly payments on a depreciating asset and service. If I ever need to sell my car due to a lowered income, I will not hesitate to do it.

Here are some useful tips to help you own what you need and achieve longer-lasting joy:

1. Before making a purchase, stop and think: "why?", don't keep anything in your house that is neither useful nor beautiful. To be happy, we must let go of our worldly possessions.
2. Value your space. Each new item you bring into your life takes up space, which takes away your space.
3. The amount of stuff you own is limited by the amount of space you have to keep it. If you live in a small apartment, you will have less space to keep stuff. This does not mean that you should buy more if you have a large home. You want to decrease the number of items in your home; that requires your time and your attention.
4. "He who knows he has enough is rich" - Lao Tzu. Basically, stop buying and wanting shit you don't need.
5. Focus on what you have, rather than what you don't have, and you'll be happier.
6. Every action has an equal and opposite reaction. Each time we buy something, there is an impact on the world, either through resource depletion, human hardship, or waste. Limiting our purchases to essentials is the best way to curb our buying, and as we reduce our consumption to save the world, our homes will stay clean and lean.

The best way to minimize is to start over. When I moved, it gave me a clean slate. It allowed me to start anew and do things right. For me, starting over was actually cheap. I was able to sell a lot of things I did not use or that were a bit on the

FINDING HAPPINESS IN THE FACE OF SUFFERING

excessive side, for example, a lounge suite when all I needed was a beautiful 3-seater couch. I was able to replace many of my old items with essential but even more decorative items.

In a case where you are settled and obviously cannot just start over as I did, you can deal with the duplicate items in your home first. Eliminate anything you're less likely to use. Yes, Elimifuckingnate! That word means to altogether remove or get rid of (something) and not look back. I just made that up.

Your home should consist only of the following items:

1. Items in your inner space. These are things that you often use which you put in places that are most easy to reach. Examples of these items are your toothbrush, laptop, and kettle.
2. Items in your outer space. These are items that you do not often use. They are possessions that you will keep on shelves, upper cabinets, and under the bed. The outer space can be used to store clothes, toilet paper, detergent, crockery, etc.

Surfaces are not for storage; they are for activities. So keep them clean and clear because visibly clear surfaces are not only attractive but are also more hygienic.

Set limits.

- Limiting commitments and activities can give you more time to work on your happiness and your goals.

- Limiting spending will reduce your credit card debts and increase your bank balance.

- Limiting fatty foods and sugar intake will improve your health and reduce your waistline.

- Limiting your space for stuff helps you develop a one-in-one-out principle that ensures that when a new item comes into your home, one piece must leave.

All of these things add to our stress. The benefits of setting limits are for a more straightforward, more abundant, healthier, and happier life. There is no master list as to what you should have as a minimalist because we are all different. What's important to us can differ based on our gender, cultures, interests, and the family members we live with.

Lastly, becoming a minimalist is not just about getting rid of stuff and having fewer things. To remain a minimalist, you need to develop a minimalist mentality and maintain a minimalist lifestyle. You need to declutter your digital life. Get off mailing lists, cancel subscriptions, avoid multitasking. Be mindful of seemingly lovely activities, such as gifting during Christmas and participating in gift exchanges. Instead, suggest activities that could better the lives of others. If you really must buy, how about you buy and give to the less fortunate or donate to the less fortunate for Christmas?

I remember the first time my mother came to visit me and saw my minimalist lifestyle; she mistook it for a "needs stuff"

FINDING HAPPINESS IN THE FACE OF SUFFERING

situation. Honestly, I found it hard but did my best to explain to her that I chose this lifestyle and had all the things I needed. Being a caring mum, she went and still got me extra hand towels anyway 😄. Mums ❤. The hand towels went to the "give things away" box. The lesson here; be ruthless in protecting your space and happiness.

Minimalism will not solve all your problems. You can be a minimalist and still have a drudgery life. Chucking away your material stuff does not equate to a happy life. It doesn't work this way in real life, unfortunately. However, minimalism will help you live a simple life and when you get rid of stuff you don't need - with a simple life, you will be able to genuinely choose who and what you want in your life. The best part about minimalist living is that the reward is almost immediate. Do it daily, and you will feel lighter, a bit happier, and pretty fantastic!

The Power Of Habits

In order to change my life, I had to change my habits. Habits are the compound interest of self-improvement. Habits are formed because the brain is always looking for the easiest way to perform a task while using as little brainpower as possible, hence it stores patterns when you do repetitive tasks over some time. This is to free up the mind to allow your brain to learn other things. The parts of the brain that store habits as patterns are called the basal ganglia. The basal ganglia are a group of structures linked to the thalamus in the base of the brain. They are involved in the coordination of movement. If you are familiar with patterns, you'll know that patterns are repeatable designs that become predictable. So the basal ganglia part of the brain stores our repeated actions as patterns in the brain, and those patterns become reusable, which is what we end up calling habits. Have you ever tried to form a habit? If you have, you'll know that habits can be hard to form, and they are also hard to break. In this chapter, I will teach you how habits are formed and how you can form habits easier.

One thing I can tell you is that every habit was once a choice. Charles Duhigg, the author of "The Power of Habit," describes a simple neurological loop at the core of every habit. This loop consists of three parts: A cue, a routine, and a reward. When you understand these elements, it can help you understand how to change bad habits or form better ones.

The section below, which explains the elements of the habit loop, was extracted from habitica.fandom.com.

"The cue for a habit can be anything that triggers the habit. Cues most generally fall under the following categories: a location, a time of day, other people, an emotional state, or an immediately preceding action. For example, every day at 2:30 pm, someone could crave chocolate from the vending machine in the other building, or the smell from the coffee house downstairs compels someone to get a latte. As another example, the music from roving ice cream trucks is a potent cue. The cue tells the brain to go into automatic processing mode, and it takes effort to resist the cue, versus deriving satisfaction from following the cue.

A habit's routine is the most prominent element. It's the behaviour you wish to change—for example, smoking or biting your nails. Or reinforce—for instance, taking the stairs instead of the elevator or drinking water instead of snacking.

The reward is the reason the brain decides the previous steps are worth remembering for the future. The compensation provides positive reinforcement for the desired behaviour, making it more likely that you will produce that behaviour again in the future. The reward can be anything, from something tangible— for example, chocolate. Something intangible— for instance, a half-hour of television to something with no inherent value but what it is given like tokens."

Habits can either bring positive or negative consequences into our lives. The thing about habits is that they are hard to get rid of. To get rid of a habit, you first need to be aware of the effect the habit has on your life. Whether it is a positive or negative

FINDING HAPPINESS IN THE FACE OF SUFFERING

effect. The reason why this is important is that habits are often so ingrained in our lives that they override our common sense and logic. The brain can perform unconscious actions without thought, so being aware of the effect and creating even the slightest shift in a routine can cause you to break a habit.

The goal of this book is to help you to become the happiest version of yourself. To become the happiest version of yourself, you must form new routines and develop new habits. To develop new habits, you must get rid of some old ones. I know this is easier said than done, which is why I am going to tell you about some of the transformational techniques that have been tried and tested to induce habit change.

You can create habits through tiny persistent steps over time. Those small decisions or steps will then compound into growth. When you want to create a habit, focus on the habits, not the goal you want to achieve. This is because winners and losers have the same goals, they all want to win. What often sets winners and losers apart are their daily habits. Are your habits contributing to your growth, success, and happiness or holding you back?

You cannot just overcome a habit. You can only change it when you can perform a new routine to cues that you are already accustomed to getting a reward for. So, if you already have a cue and routine for which you get rewarded, you need to form a new routine for the same cue so that you get the reward you need.

Before I go further, I need to highlight "belief". A factor that comes into play to change a habit is belief. When you have belief, it makes habit change possible. Your belief can be in a higher power, it can be in a drug, a ritual, or it can be in a person. It doesn't matter what you believe in because belief is belief. You must believe that you can change your habit. If you do not believe that you can change your habits, then you probably won't be able to change your habits. Many of us have limiting beliefs that hold us back from achieving the things we are capable of in our lives. For your habits to change, you have to believe that you can change them.

To make a habit change effective, you must identify and change a keystone habit. Changing one keystone habit can lead to a chain reaction of other habit changes. In my case, in 2018, on 7 January, I stopped drinking Alcohol. Although I never drank on weekdays, I used to leisure-drink on Fridays and Saturdays. Drinking was a weekend habit. Every Friday afternoon, I'd find myself at Makro liquors, reading the back of different wine bottles and looking for a new craft beer to try out. I drank any type of good quality alcohol brand I could find, but I loved dry red wines. So, I would visit the same liquor stores every Friday for wines, craft gin, or craft beer, etc. It was a habit. Friday was my cue, going to the liquor store was the routine, wine or craft beer was my reward. So for me, quitting alcohol was a keystone habit that caused a chain reaction and caused other habits to change. Which resulted in me putting a stop to my weekly Friday trips to the liquor stores.

Alcohol consumption usually led to going out to restaurants and clubs, which led to money-wastage and not-so-ethical

FINDING HAPPINESS IN THE FACE OF SUFFERING

decision-making. It led to finding myself in situations that I otherwise wouldn't be in if I had just stayed at home. Alcohol led to me being surrounded by some people that added zero value towards my life's goals. Except to waste time and teach me a valuable lesson about getting nothing and an experience on ways to spend time in a futile manner.

Quitting alcohol, putting an end to money wastage through alcohol consumption, and discovering non-alcohol-related activities have led to more responsible behaviour. It stopped me from being involved in messy situations with drunk people. It made it easier to cut off certain people from my life and left me with people that are meant to be in my life and meet new people for the next chapter of my life. I no longer wasted my weekends on drinking and associated activities. Instead, I spend it with family and on occasion, with close friends, but most often, just with myself, relaxing and working on my future. This book you are reading was written by me on weekends, thanks to the time I created for myself through changing one keystone habit of stopping alcohol consumption.

Another keystone habit of mine that changed my life was the habit of reading. Since I started making reading books a keystone habit, many areas of my life have changed. Usually, I'd watch videos, but when I switched to audiobooks, I watched fewer videos. Reading books helped me make a radical transformation that led to me being the happiest person I know. It has led to my companies growing and career growth. It has led to me being able to make a valuable contribution to the world than I could ever have imagined without reading.

By establishing a keystone habit to stop drinking, and to read more regularly; I was able to develop other keystone habits, such as waking up at 4 am every morning instead of 7:30 am, and sometimes at 9:00 am. The reason I decided to wake up this early was so I could have time in my mornings for more reading, which then led to time for meditation, cleaning, and exercise. Changing one keystone habit, such as waking up earlier, meant that I slept earlier at night. Which is obviously more manageable because I don't go out to party late. This also meant that I now had time in the mornings to do the above-mentioned things I've always desired to do but never created time for.

Meditation has improved several areas of my life, which I will discuss in the chapter dedicated to meditation. I run in the morning because it contributes to my happiness and health. It helps with dopamine release, which puts me in a good mood at the start of my day, and it keeps me healthy and in good shape. This helps set the tone for how I start my day and how I want the rest of it to go. The reading made me more knowledgeable about improving certain areas of my life. It helped me be more impactful to those around me. This was what led me to write this book, being active on social media, starting a podcast, growing my businesses, and so on. All of this started with changing keystone habits.

My ultimate goal for quitting alcohol, starting to read; and all the habits that were developed along the way, was to reach the ultimate victory of living a happier, healthier, and financially successful life. Changing one keystone habit caused other habits to form and add up into the final victory. A vital step

FINDING HAPPINESS IN THE FACE OF SUFFERING

to maintaining keystone habits is recognising them and appreciating how far you have come from that one change in your life. Recognising a keystone habit will prevent you from repeating it even when times get tough. This is when most people start to regress into old habits that cause more harm than good. What keystone habit do you have that you think is currently doing you more harm than good and holding you back from reaching your goals? Identify this habit, write it down and love yourself enough to put an end to it.

Another habit I developed in the mornings is making my bed every morning as I wake up. This habit is associated with higher productivity.

While I got to form some habits because it was a decision that made absolute sense, this one was because I had contemplated the decision for some time. For example, quitting alcohol. It was a decision that I had considered for a few months, and it was an easy decision to make. There are other habits, such as sleeping earlier at night because I woke up at 4 am that required willpower. Willpower is a compelling ability to have to help us reach our goals and to form habits. Without willpower, I could not have gotten into bed at 9 pm although my natural clock wants me to sleep at 1 am and wake up at 7 am. Willpower is what makes me get out of bed within 10 minutes of my alarm going off at 4 am and start my day while it is still dark when most people I know are still sleeping. Having high willpower is associated with a greater chance of success in life.

To test willpower, an experiment was performed on toddlers based on a study from 1972 which was led by psychologist

Walter Mischel, a professor at Stanford University. In this study, a child was offered a choice between one small but immediate reward, or two small rewards if they waited for a period of time.

This experiment has since been replicated by parents where toddlers are left alone with a bowl of marshmallows and are instructed not to eat the marshmallows until their parents came back to test their willpower. This experiment showed that kids with higher willpower resisted eating the marshmallows. This test concluded that the kids that resisted until their parents came back and let them have some sweets had higher willpower and were more likely to be successful in life. Despite this research, I believe that willpower can be developed and strengthened over time.

We are solely responsible for our habits. Even habits that turn into bad addictions. Every addict is responsible for their habits. This is because every habit starts as a choice. It begins with a decision to one day do something such as smoke a cigarette, cheat on your spouse, try a drug, have a glass of alcohol, go to the casino to gamble, or gamble from home.

The same way choices can result in bad habits, they can also result in good habits. You are conscious of most of the habits you currently have in your life. When you sleep, when you wake up, when you eat, when you work, when you study, when you go to work, etc. When you realise that habits result from a choice and that they can change, then you'll realise that you have the power to remake them. Believing in change is a superpower. Believing that you have the power to change and remake your habits while making that belief a habit is how powerful a habit can be.

A habit is created when you have something you are looking forward to upon creating the pattern. A lot of times, you are not aware of a habit. Still, when you become conscious of a habit and can identify what triggers that habit, that's when you gain the power to change it. Changing a habit can be difficult, but with enough desire to change the habit and with a small shift in mindset and routine, you can change any habit. It is now time to use habits to become a better and happier individual. Use habits to take control of your life, your time, and your happiness.

All big things come from small beginnings. When you want to form a habit, always remember why you wanted to form that habit in the first place and then focus on the systems that will get you to your why. Your systems are the small repeatable actions you need to take every day that compound into a habit and give you the results you want. Your reason for forming a habit is usually to reach a goal, but you should not focus on the target daily. Instead, focus on the small repeatable actions you need to do, and you will get to your goal.

Here are some habits you want to create:

- You want to develop a habit of getting 7 - 9 hours' sleep every day for better mental health

- you want to develop a habit of prioritising making meals or a grocery list so that you can eat 3 times a day plus exercise for physical health

- you want to create a habit of meditating or praying every day for mental and spiritual growth

- you want to develop a habit of reading for mental growth

- you want to build a habit of writing down and visualising your goals so that it becomes easier to reach them.

- you want to prioritise a habit of having peace of mind.

Design your environment to meet your needs. A huge factor that will contribute to your success in forming new habits is your environment. You can set yourself up for success when you change your environment to meet your needs. If you want to exercise daily, have your running shoes out and/or exercise mats where you can easily see them.

I will now share with you how you can make your habits easier, enjoyable, and rewarding for yourself. If you want to keep doing the exercise, make sure it is an exercise you enjoy. Don't run if you hate running. There are so many different types of exercise you can explore. The trick to creating a new habit is to make habit-forming easier. What is rewarded is repeated and what is punished is deserted. Your habit should feel rewarding, not punishing. Do the exercise you love. If you want to eat healthily, eat the fruits you like. If you want to read, read only the books you enjoy. As much as I enjoy reading books for knowledge, there are some books written by some of the most

FINDING HAPPINESS IN THE FACE OF SUFFERING

renowned authors in the world which millions of people rave about that I could not even get past the first three pages because I simply did not enjoy them. I would like to thank you for reading this far into my book. This tells me that you are really enjoying the book and that you are learning from it. I hope it gives you all the knowledge you need to make a radical transformation in your life.

Meditation can be boring, but I meditate. Unlike the boring meditation where you feel like you have been meditating for ages when in fact, you have only closed your eyes for two minutes. The type of meditation I perform lets my thoughts flow but keeps them focused on conscious intents and I sometimes find that 40 minutes have passed. I had previously learned that the old method of meditating through complete mind stillness initially just wasn't for me because I could not still my mind. However, I grew to learn how to still my mind for a few minutes at a time. To make meditation a habit and a habit I love, I needed to find a type of meditation that worked for me. Don't worry, I will introduce you to this meditation that has worked for me in the next chapter. I am confident that it will work for you too, especially if you have had trouble with the old tedious meditation method. Make good habits more comfortable and more rewarding. If you are satisfied with the reward of a habit, you will want more. The opposite is exact for bad habits. Make bad habits harder for yourself, unattractive, and unpleasant.

You also want to apply the Goldilocks Rule to help you form new habits. The Goldilocks Rule states that humans experience peak motivation when working on tasks that are right on the edge of their current abilities. You don't want to start a new habit on an extreme of too hard or too easy. You want to start on a "just right" level of comfort and progress. Take, for example, myself, with writing this book. It was hard to start writing this book when I focused on just completing the book. It only became easy when I concentrated on writing one paragraph a day, then one page a day, then 2000 words a day, and so on. After many days of writing on a "just right" level, I found myself with a whole book written out.

Let me give another example of when you are playing a computer game. Have you ever tried to jump into a car-racing game where some guys are driving really fast and seem good at it? If you did try, you'd find that you'd probably suck and crash everywhere. The game would not be challenging for the "master" of the game if they played with you. They probably wouldn't want to play with you, and you'd probably not be eager to play against them again or even play the game at all because you sucked. But, if you decide to play the game on a beginner level, at a slower speed and setting, you'll find yourself being in a better position to control the cars. You'd be in a better position to win against a master in the game yet, the beginner level would be too dull for a master. The point of this is to illustrate the "just right" level. As a beginner into something, you should start on a beginner's level. In the case of a car-racing video game, if you play on the beginner level and move up the levels, you can easily play like a master within two weeks of playing the game. It's amazing, but that's just how quickly the mind learns and adapts. And when you get to this

FINDING HAPPINESS IN THE FACE OF SUFFERING

master level, a beginner level will no longer be challenging, and you won't be motivated to play with a beginner.

The Goldilocks principle helps people stay motivated in life and in business. When you challenge yourself on a "just right" level, you will be rewarded and feel inclined to repeat the routine. As you repeat the routine, you will get better and better. Until one day, you find yourself at a master's level. How can you apply the Goldilocks Rule in your own life? Try it on something, not too hard and not too easy, on something "just right".

You can make forming habits easier by bundling the habits you need to do with the habits you want to do. An example of a habit I needed was the habit of exercising, and the habit I wanted was to have an excellent breakfast in the morning. So what I did was that I would not eat until I had exercised. On a busy morning, the exercise could be a quick 40 x push-ups for one minute, and then I'd eat.

Another example is my morning meditation and having my morning coffee. Meditation is the habit I need and drinking coffee is that habit I want. I then make sure that I meditate (a habit I need) first, and then I have my morning coffee (a habit I want).

If you want to get started with forming a new habit, you first need clarity on "why" you need to form the habit, and, "what" habit it is that you want to establish. You will then need to set a time of day for "when" that habit will occur and "where" that habit will take place. In other words, you need to have a clear "why", "what", "when", and "where". For example, when I wanted to start exercising daily, my "why" was that I wanted to become happier and healthier because exercising helps you secrete dopamine. Dopamine is associated with improved moods and increased happiness. I then told myself that I would exercise in the mornings after my morning coffee, which was my "when"—the "where" was on the beach.

Here's another example; when I wanted to start meditating, my "why" was that I wanted to raise my self-awareness and reprogram my mind for happiness. Because meditating helps you become more self-aware and with the conscious intent involved in meditation, you can reprogram your brain. It will propel you forward in life. I then told myself that I would meditate in the mornings before my first cup of coffee, which was my 'when'—the 'where' was on my couch. To be honest, I tried to meditate in many places before I settled on the sofa. I tried it on the floor and found the floor too hard. I tried it in the car, but that was also uncomfortable. I tried it on my balcony and actually liked that. I tried it with my legs crossed, and my knees were super sore after I finished. The point here is that your 'where' is up to you.

So when you identify your "why", then the behaviour you need to develop for it and set a time and place, you will be more likely to move forward with that habit.

The question now is: "how do you make sure that you can maintain the new habits you will form after reading this book?" The answer is through habit tracking. As humans, we are very visual animals. We are motivated to do more when we are seen.

FINDING HAPPINESS IN THE FACE OF SUFFERING

It's something that has been a part of us since we were children. Have you noticed a toddler will look at you when they are playing, and if they see you looking at them, they play even harder? As humans, we are motivated to stay on course with our habits when we can track our progress. If you want to run, track your kilometres per week or miles per week if you live in America. If you are on a weight loss diet, track your weight every day or weekly. If you meditate, you will just start feeling great. I wish I could tell you about an app you can use to track your meditation, but I don't use one. I just started feeling really amazing, and that was all the motivation I needed to continue.

The most important thing to remember about forming habits is to focus on just starting and taking that first step. Don't overthink it or focus on the outcome. It's all about what you do today and tomorrow and the day after. The compound of your daily habits will happen daily. You just need to focus on the start and doing, not the end. Small daily improvements are the key to staggering long-term results.

Set Long-Term Goals

To set long-term goals, you have to be truly honest with yourself about what you really want, because we repeatedly tell ourselves what we think we want. Do you know what you want? Do you know what you truly want? Because a lot of us think we just want a better car, a better house, a better job, but most of us do not really know what we truly want from life. What we think we truly want from life are often things that we believe will make us look good in the eyes of others. We want what our peers tell us we should desire. We want what our upbringing tells us we should want. We want our fantasies. We repeat these things in our minds, and they blur what we genuinely want and desire, which is to be fucking happy.

- Goal Setting as We Know It Is Broken

Our thoughts shape our actions, our goals help to develop our ideas, and our goals are shaped by our mindset.

If we change our mindset, we'll be able to set goals that align with our happiness and passions. When we set goals that align with our joy and our desires, we'll be consistent as fuck with our choices and actions. Remember, we are responsible for our decisions.

This is how important setting goals can shape your life. When you set goals to be happy, the choices to do things that make you satisfied become much more manageable. You'll start to think more and do more of the things that make you happy. You'll read more about the foods that are good for your body and mind and do more activities that make you happy. While we're on this topic, remember that happiness is cultivated through love, selflessness, gratitude, forgiveness, and kindness. Being loving, kind, selfless, thankful, and forgiving will make you happy physiologically, and it will make being around you pleasant for the people close to you. It will improve your relationships and increase your influence. Everyone just wants to feel important, and that's how you increase your influence. By making others feel important through sincere appreciation, kindness, selflessness, and love. Being selfless is another word for giving to others without looking for personal gain. If you give time, money, or things to other people without expecting something in return, that's selfless. So simple, yet a lot of people miss the significance of being a genuinely compassionate person. The universe will align in your favour, and you will be happier.

There are times when you have to make conflicting decisions on your happiness, such as being asked to do something you do not really want to do. In these situations, saying 'No' may seem unkind or selfish. Still, you are allowed to say "No" when something does not align with your happiness. That act of saying "No" is an act of self-love. When happiness is a goal, you will not worry about saying "No" to others. It is how you say "No" that matters because you can say "No" and still be kind.

We are responsible for our choices, and the choices we make shape our lives. A decision to say "No" when something will make you unhappy is a choice to saying yes to your happiness. This is why it is essential to have long-term life goals to be happy. These goals serve as our true north and guide our

FINDING HAPPINESS IN THE FACE OF SUFFERING

choices. Our long-term happiness goals should cover every essential aspect of our lives: our careers or/and businesses, our relationships, our bodies, our minds, our spirituality. Yes, I did not include money because the money will come when you set your purpose and align it with your passion.

Here's a rule for setting your purpose within your goal setting; It should be based on your actions because those are the only things you can truly control. Let me say this in another way: Don't base your purpose on the activities of other people. Your mission is your contribution to others which you feel passionate about, but it should not be linked to the actions of someone else. Your goals cannot be founded on the actions of other people because that is their own universe, which is in their own control, not yours.

I have goals for my happiness, which is why I meditate and exercise. Meditation helps me with my cultivation of joy, and the exercise helps with my secretion of endorphins, which makes me happy throughout my day.

I have goals for my mental and physical health, which is also why I exercise. When I set goals for my health, my body fat dropped because I worked out more and ate healthier. I became more aware of the foods I put in my mouth and exercise no longer felt like a chore. My health and body goals had become a passion that allowed me to remain consistent.

I set goals for my relationships with close friends and family to be more appreciative. So I started to show more appreciation for having them in my life and began to be more present in theirs. Do you notice how this goal has nothing to do with their actions? Remember that everyone just wants to feel important, and you can make people feel important through sincere appreciation and kindness. You cannot control the actions of others, but you can influence their actions towards you. It can all start with the choices you make and the steps you take.

I set career goals that are very important because I want to do something I am passionate about; this involves solving problems. The problem I have chosen to address is the unhappiness problem. Yes, I decided to solve unhappiness. It sounds crazy writing this, but that's a problem I saw is plaguing the world and the problem I have chosen to address. When you solve problems, people will pay you for them.

- Goals For My Mind

To solve this problem, I had to keep upgrading my mind. I have to continue reading and consuming as much knowledge about happiness as possible. I had to research and then start to take action steps. I needed to reach as many people as possible with my message. I needed to create a product that I have never done before, such as writing a book. Then I researched how to write a book. Yes, I read three books on how to write a book before writing this book. I followed media experts in the field of personal growth and personal development such as Vishen Lakiani, Jim Kwik, and Tony Robbins amongst many others. I downloaded and listened to audiobook-based masterclasses on joy, the awakening of the mind, happiness, and purpose. All of this was because of my goals. My point is this: when you

FINDING HAPPINESS IN THE FACE OF SUFFERING

set purposeful goals, your thoughts and actions become your passion, and you will be able to stay focused and on track.

It is imperative to set happiness as a goal before career goals because a happy you will help guide your progression in your career. You will have a higher IQ when you are content and be better equipped to make the right decisions about what you truly want to do with your life. An increase in IQ increases your ability to learn, hence, you will learn faster and thirst for more knowledge. Not only that, but you'll have better influence and be a better leader. The people you work with will find you more accessible to work with. Finally, happy people do better work and are more productive.

Every choice you make will either contribute to your happiness or not. It will help you have better relationships or not. It will add to growing us spiritually or not. It will contribute to you having better health and mindset or not. Your choices either make you better or detract from you, yet the time and effort are the same. The option is yours.

- What Do You Really Want from Life?

To determine what you really want from life, you need to start with your "Why?"

- What makes you come alive? Do that.

- How do you want your life to be measured?

- What inspires you?

- What lights a fire in your belly?

- Where can you add the highest value?

- If money wasn't an issue, what would you do?

- What past signposts can you use to define your future? What made you tick as a child? What did you enjoy doing?

To set and achieve your goals, you can meditate, or you can perform a simple exercise that will require you to have a total commitment. I will talk about meditation later, but for now, I will share an activity that you can practice. It is quite a straightforward exercise. Once you have answers to the questions above, you will need to write down a goals list, then you will need to look at this list in the morning, at midday, and before sleeping at night. It must be all you think about almost obsessively. Please do not share this list with anyone because you do not want any negativity that might influence your thoughts or plant a seed of doubt, then work steadily each day towards these goals and very importantly, express gratitude every time you see results. That's the exercise you can practice if you prefer not to meditate.

> - Our Mind Is Our Most Potent Weapon as Humans Because Our Thoughts Literally Shape Our Universe.

I am going to get a little geeky in the next few paragraphs, so please stay with me. Back in 2016 up till 2019, I spent a lot of time learning about quantum physics to try and understand the universe better. Quantum physics is the fundamental theory in physics describing the properties of nature on an atomic scale. Basically, the stuff that happens in the atomic and subatomic levels. This is because the physics laws that govern what we see and feel, do not rule the physics within the quantum realm. And within this realm, nothing is decided until you decide that it is. Basically, what I am saying is that your future is pretty much undecided until your thoughts and actions determine what will happen. Many probable futures are waiting for you, and it is up to your ideas and activities to shape your universe because that power belongs to you. I will give an example of this power using quantum physics as an example:

In quantum physics, a subatomic particle is said to have the ability to be in multiple states at the same time until it is measured or observed. What this means is; there are numerous probable finite positions of a subatomic particle, and the absolute position of a subatomic particle is decided after the particle is observed by a human. So, basically, at the subatomic level, our thoughts and focus on a particle will determine its "real" position. Just like your thoughts, focus, and action will determine your future.

Here's the thing, subatomic particles make up our universe and everything- EVERYTHING! And if human thought and observation can decide the position of a subatomic particle, imagine the impact the human mind has on shaping the world collectively in the quantum realm, which essentially makes up our physical world. The human mind shapes our reality and the world we live in. It's still a bit of a less understood science;

however, it is common sense that the choices we make, shape our lives.

There's a simple exercise that you can perform to harness the power of the mind. This was developed by a man named Neville Goddard. He was a mystical writer and lecturer who taught us that everything we see and experience individually, is a product of everything that happens in our own dream of reality. He taught us that through a combination of emotional conviction and mental images, each person can imagine their own world into being.

The exercise in harnessing the power of the mind to imagine your world into being is described by Neville Goddard in three simple steps:

- Step 1: Clarify your desire

- Step 2: Sit still or lie down in a deeply relaxed state, similar to what you'd experience just before you go to sleep

- Step 3: Visualise or see in your mind your desire being fulfilled such as someone congratulating you or giving you an award and you're holding the award. Feel the emotions you'll feel when you achieve this desire. Emotions help make the visual experience more productive.

Each time I tell people about these three steps, I see two types of reactions: a nodding head to signal agreement, and I also see doubt. The truth is: most people will not do these exercises because they simply do not comprehend the power of the mind. Most people would not be caught dead using philosophy

FINDING HAPPINESS IN THE FACE OF SUFFERING

like this to help them focus on their goals. This is not imagination, it is action. The action of you visualising what you genuinely want is a step toward focusing on and achieving your long-term goals. Your directed will mental activity generates a physical force, which is the reality in which you live.

Now, let me ask you this; did you set happiness as a goal? Did you set "peace of mind" as a goal? If you do not have these written down as your goals, how do you expect to take daily consistent actions to ensure that you live in a beautiful state? Here's the thing, a lot of people say they will be happy when they get a job, when they get a promotion, when they become rich, when; when; when. For millions of people around the world that are living happy lives, being happy is an active goal. Humans are programmed to survive, not to be happy and it is up to each and every individual to make a conscious effort and choice to set happiness as a goal, learn how to, and take action toward cultivating happiness in their lives. Happiness doesn't come to us in the end. We die in the end. Happiness is not an end goal because it is always available to us in each and every moment of our lives. It is a means to assist us with achieving other goals. You have happiness in you, and it is up to you to learn how to cultivate it in your daily life.

Something To Do

The choice to change your life is presented to you every day. Do you set short-term goals? What are the things that you do every day that give you a sense of accomplishment? Something ritualistic that contributes towards reaching your long-term goals, or do you just do things every day without seeing yourself getting any closer to your long-term goals? In this chapter, we will evaluate the effectiveness and purpose of short-term goals on your long-term goals and your happiness.

You can increase your natural state of happiness by doing something that gives you meaning. It's a scientific fact: if you do this every day, you will have something to be happy about every day. We get a sense of our purpose from the long-term goals we set. Still, if we focus entirely on the long-term goals and the results, we can end up becoming stressed and depressed because we worry about our long-term goals. This worry often results in none of it actually happening. Don't get me wrong, long-term goals do happen when you work consistently towards them, but the goal post is always shifting. Your goals for the next three years will change in the next year because you are still growing. In other words, the goals you have set for yourself in three years would have changed a year from now.

One of the things that cause us to doubt ourselves, stress, and give us anxiety is focusing too much on the outcome of our long-term goals. Although it is essential to have a long-term goal to provide us with a north, it is also very critical to have mini-goals for each day that bring instant rewards.

These mini goals give a sense of purpose to each day; what I like to call our rituals. Rituals are a set of actions you perform in a fixed order. They are the best way to reach our long-term goals and allow us to live happier lives. Rituals are known to help us live longer. Rituals are how the people of the Okinawa Island of Japan go about their day.

The Okinawa Island of Japan is home to the world's oldest people per 100,000 inhabitants. Thirty-five out of every 100,000 people on Okinawa Island in Japan are over the age of 100, and the life expectancy on this Island is 83.7 years, according to the World Health Organization Statistics. The book Ikigai: The Japanese Secret Philosophy for a Happy Healthy Long Life with Joy and Purpose Every Day - That is a long-ass title for a book. In the book, one of the Japanese secret ways of adding joy, meaning, and purpose to every single day is simply never stop moving and having something to do every day. No one on the Island just sits and does nothing. They keep moving. Old people as old as over 80 take walks and ride bicycles. They tend to their gardens. They don't retire. The act of 'doing' adds a sense of purpose to each of their days.

What we have done every day has contributed to the person that we are at this moment, and what we continue to do will add to the person we become. This includes what we eat, what we read, who we associate ourselves with, and how we treat our bodies. A person who wants better health as a long-term goal should eat healthier every day and exercise. A person who wants knowledge should read more. A person who wants better understanding should write or teach. A person who

FINDING HAPPINESS IN THE FACE OF SUFFERING

wants to be happier should follow the principles described in this book.

We can learn a lot from the habits of the Okinawa Island inhabitants. For example, their eating habits are part of the things that are attributed to their longevity. They eat unprocessed foods with little meat every day; the keywords there are EVERY DAY. The traditional Okinawa diet focuses on whole foods. It consists of around 30 percent green and yellow vegetables and smaller quantities of rice compared to mainland Japanese diets. The menu features a small amount of omega 3 fatty acid-rich fish. Pork is valued highly in this diet but is eaten rarely.

We can learn from their social practices by keeping a close-knit circle of friends and having a sense of community. Most of us are fixated on our busy lives and chasing our dreams. Still, research has shown that keeping a close-knit circle of friends or family and having goals for your connection with your loved ones will make you happier. Here's the thing: you cannot control how others feel about and act towards you, but you can control how you interact with others based on your goals. For example, I plan to be the best uncle to my nephews, and I call and go to see them whenever I can. Although my goal is to be close to them, I cannot control their goals. They frankly could be indifferent whether I call or if they are close to me. My three-year-old nephew would rather watch YouTube videos than be on a video call with me, however, I am still able to have a close relationship with them. Because I take action steps within my control, such as being present, communicating, and being the best version of myself I could possibly be.

The point is, your social goals do not need to depend on the other person, if they are your kids, spouse, family, you know what your connections with them are and you can set what "connection" goals you want to have based on what you can control, which translates to your actions concerning the work you have to do on yourself. My goal is to be a present uncle, I get better at it because I work on myself. That goal makes me happy. If you have toxic people in your life and your goal is to be happy, you can reduce your exposure to those people. You can decide what type of connection you want to have with them based on your own interaction. To those with whom you wish to build a meaningful, healthy relationship: remember that everyone wants to be appreciated and made to feel important. A simple text message to a friend, saying "Hey, I know we have not spoken in a while, and I hope that you are doing great." could be all you need to say to start reconnecting, or a simple once-a-week-call or visit to see family could be a way to strengthen the connection. Love and connections are a vital part of our happiness, they should be set as part of our short-term goals as something we practice every day or as often as we can. The more we practice, the better we get at it. When you are starting something new, remember to begin slowly and gradually build up your ability, and you will get better and better over time. This is also how habits form.

Forming new habits is harder for older people than it is for young people or kids however we are all capable of forming new habits. To become a better you, you will need to develop new habits. There is a difference between what is right for you and what you want to do, this is because people - especially

FINDING HAPPINESS IN THE FACE OF SUFFERING

older people - usually want to do things the way they have always done them. The brain tries to conserve as much energy as possible. When the brain develops a habit, it doesn't want to think anymore; It does things on autopilot, and the only way to break a habit is to present the brain with new information. When you give the brain advancing information, it is revitalised. It is important to keep your mind open and expose yourself to knowledge by reading, even if this means stepping out of your comfort zone and experiencing a bit of anxiety. Challenging the brain is the best way to form habits, which will allow you to continually achieve your short-term goals. In the end, it will lead to you making your long-term goals a reality. Hard times are the universe's way of pushing you out of your comfort zone. Those who resist will suffer, while those that expose themselves to new information, let their brains be challenged, and form new habits will find happiness and joy. We should learn to recognise the beauty of our imperfections and see them as an opportunity for growth.

There are other benefits of having short-term goals, such as limiting stress, helping you build confidence, and reducing anxiety. While a little stress is right for you and can actually make you live longer according to some studies, sustaining a high level of stress is terrible for you and can lead to all sorts of health impairments. Stress and anxiety are often brought about by worry, which is an excessive obsession with a desire which can prevent that exact desire from becoming fulfilled. Having short-term goals reduces worry and fear, which reduces stress and anxiety.

A simple habit you can adopt if you find yourself stressed and anxious is to turn off your phone's internet an hour before you go to sleep. You don't want to turn it on until an hour after you wake up either. This advice is not limited to phones, it applies to your other devices, such as tablets, TV, internet glasses, etc. You can leave the mobile network on to receive calls in case you want family or friends to reach you for emergencies while leaving the internet connectivity disabled.

Other rituals you can add are Yoga and Meditation. Yoga is a mind-body practice that combines physical poses, controlled breathing, and meditation or relaxation. It may help reduce stress, lower blood pressure, and heart rate, and almost anyone can do it. I personally just do meditation with controlled breathing and visualisation.

Setting short-term goals is the easiest way to gain control over your life and become happier. If you want control over your life, you first need to gain control over your mind. I want to make it clear that the mindset alone is not a magic wand. It undoubtedly plays a role in your happiness, your health, and your wealth. We don't live under just the "laws of attraction", which state that you can attract whatever it is that you focus on. Although the mind has a central role to play in reaching our goals, we must use all the resources available to us: educational, mental, physical, and financial. I feel strongly against books and teachers that hand people an over-promise of just one of the laws with guarantees: these books that state that all you need is to focus your mind, or that all you need is capital, or to take action. Don't rely on a single method, saying affirmations alone without work will not get you anywhere. A positive

FINDING HAPPINESS IN THE FACE OF SUFFERING

mindset without skills will not get you far. No matter how much you visualise and train, without the physical abilities of Usain Bolt, you will not become the fastest man on earth.

Skills are everything and the skills people often learn are the skills required for their work because most people want to get better at their work, but most people do not spend time learning the skills needed for living a happy life. I am going to teach you the skills that you can use every day that will allow you to live a much more comfortable life.

The only thing you can truly control is your mind. For those who want to live a more comfortable and happier life, the secret is to gain control over the things you CAN control, which is control of your mind.

When your goal is to make money quickly:

So many things in the world are marketed as easy. Examples are bitcoin trading, trading forex, drop shipping, etc. But if you ask the people who have tried any of these things, over 90% will tell you that they lost money and that they do not do it anymore. If these things are easy, then what's the problem? What a lot of people do not realise is that these things are simply a hack to make money quickly, but what they do not realise is that to master a hack, a lot of work needs to go in. In preparation for the execution of these hacks. Lots of reading, lots of learning, studying, mentorship, etc is required.

Some people get lucky while others prepare. Luck is a chance; you can increase your chances with preparation. If you do not prepare yourself for happiness, your chances of living a happy

life are slim. Where does happiness come from? When your goal is to be happier, you need to hack your mind: your brain.
◇

So why do you think you'll just get lucky and live a beautiful life unless you prepare your mind for happiness? The question now is: how can you make it easy to be happy every day? By gaining control of your mindset so that you can gain control over your life.

You can easily hack your mind by programming your brain for happiness. The requirements for hacking your mindset are the same as the requirements needed to be good at anything. The condition is simple: it requires self-discipline, and for me, discipline is the highest form of self-love. Something everyone successful in an area of their life knows too well is that you need self-discipline in order to be successful. You'll need "self-discipline" to perform the next steps I'm about to share with you. If you have self-discipline, you can be good at anything you want to do in life, including hacking your mind to happiness.

When you're faced with big goals, break them up into rituals which are small steps. You should not stress about the outcomes. Happiness is in the doing, not in the result, in other words, focus on performing consistent rituals over obsessing over the goals because there is happiness in the "doing".

- Build Confidence with Small Improvements Over Time

FINDING HAPPINESS IN THE FACE OF SUFFERING

Setting short-term goals daily followed by action helps with the building of self-confidence, and it will help you reach your goals. If you are worried about being consistent? Passion for what you do will make you consistent as hell. This is why we are told to do what we have a passion for because it is just so much easier to remain consistent. Consistency over time will make you confident and help you reach your goals.

I admire Conor McGregor for his accomplishment in the ring. Conor McGregor was quoted saying, "I'm not different than I was before, I just was committed and worked hard and earned it, that's it. We are all equal and it's the work you're willing to put in and the commitment you are willing to put in.", I must say that we are not all equal, however, we all have something we can be great at.

Conor McGregor is one of the most successful mixed martial art and boxer in the world today. When he's asked about his confidence and his success, he says it's because of his work ethic. He has a Kaizen approach to mastering his craft. What is Kaizen? Kaizen means that you have a personal commitment to continuous never-ending improvement. So instead of working hard for 2 weeks and go "oh shit, this isn't working" and then just giving up, you instead focus on those tiny daily improvements that lead to an immense reward over time. You see, your focus is not next year, it is today. Imagine each day where you improve your craft like a bricklayer where each day you just lay one brick over each other, not three, not ten. One day, brick by brick, and then one day you will have a skyscraper, then soon enough, that skyscraper is kissing the clouds and the world is at your feet. That is the result of Kaizen. This is how short-term daily goals should be approached; by focusing your actions on the little things and then remaining consistent over time.

Another example of the Kaizen effect is with Arnold Schwarzenegger. He did not kick his way out of his mother with all the muscle that led him to win all those international bodybuilding championships, he exercised increasingly with heavyweights, and every day his muscles got more prominent. After some years, he was at world-champion level. Lifting weights every day to gain muscles did not start with Arnold; Milo, an ancient Greek athlete, lifted a calf every day and carried it a short distance, four years later, he was still carrying the same calf, but he gained immortal fame because four years later, this calf had grown into a bull. I don't think anyone else has pulled off that stunt since, now I'm not suggesting that you should start lifting a calf every day to build self-confidence, although it would definitely make you stronger. The Kaizen principle works for developing your confidence in much simpler and more natural ways. What you need to do is to make a decision that you will take a specific action to build your self-confidence in a particular area and then do it.

Select a relatively easy goal to accomplish and then proceed until you reach it. Every time you complete a task, and it goes successfully, celebrate and congratulate yourself. This is the power that lies in setting those short-term goals every single day. How I like to set my short-term daily goals is through visual meditation. I will discuss visual meditation in the next chapter with an activity that will help you accomplish your short-term goals/daily plans more easily.

FINDING HAPPINESS IN THE FACE OF SUFFERING

Building muscles can help you get to champion-level. Reaching your higher goal, which is the more difficult task, that is: 'After I have these muscles'. What is the long-term goal? To be a world champion - that is the long-term goal. But what does he have to do every day? Go to the gym and build those muscles. You build up the amount of weight gradually and run more swiftly, and before long, you'll be doing things that you never thought you could. You would have acquired the self-confidence you will need to succeed in whatever you desire, and more often than not, you would have done everything to help you succeed.

Meditation

Life is created twice. It is first created in your mind and then in reality. The tool to mindfully create is meditation. It is the "what". It is a tool that you can use to help you reprogram your brain, stay focused on a goal, become more self-aware, spiritual, resilient, cope with stress and reduce anxiety. Meditation is one of the fastest ways to evolve your brain. When you start to meditate, you are first taught how to breathe. This is because breathing can be used to control your mood and lower your stress. When you breathe deeply and slowly, it sends a message to your brain to calm down. There is no magic to it. It works because it allows more air into your chest cavity, which flows into your body to help you calm your nerves, reducing stress and anxiety.

A type of meditation I do to quickly calm my nerves, especially when I am on my way to speak in front of an audience is breathing meditation. Learning breathing meditation is very useful because it can be practiced at any time, even with people around. You can do it while sitting on a chair or the floor, and even while driving. Slow deep breathing works by:

- Step 1: inhaling slowly while counting from zero to four in your mind

- Step 2: then holding your breath while counting to four

- Step 3: then exhale while counting to four and

- Step 4: then hold again while counting to four

- Step 5: repeat.

The slow deep breathing meditation technique can also quickly get you into a meditative state for other meditation techniques.

The benefits of meditation are plentiful. Meditation itself won't awaken you; however, it helps to strengthen you mentally, change you physiologically, and deepen your understanding of life. Many people meditate and then think they are not good at meditating because their minds drift off, but that is what your mind is programmed to do. Your mind will drift, and each time you catch yourself and bring your mind back to the still point of focus, then my friend, you have trained your mind for that session, that's one of the effectiveness of meditation; to train the mind to become more aware and be more present.

For meditation to work effectively, you first need a deeper understanding of why you are meditating. If you do not understand the "why", you will simply get bored and add meditation to the list of things you tried and didn't work. Before you start to meditate, ask yourself, "Have I taken responsibility for who I am and all the decisions I have made in my life to lead me to where I am?". Have you accepted full responsibility for your own life and accepted that your thoughts, desires, and actions have shaped your life up until now? You must accept that your thoughts, desires, and actions will continue to shape your life from here onward until you die.

When you accept responsibility and remain conscious of your power to create your life, your action to meditate will adapt your mind to help you set a foundation for preparing yourself

FINDING HAPPINESS IN THE FACE OF SUFFERING

to build the life you want. However, if your reason for meditating is to just try out something you think might make you happy but have not yet accepted that your thoughts, desires, and actions shape your world and your reality, then you will be wasting your time with meditation. In fact, let me not say "waste your time", the truth is that meditation will always be effective, however, the level of effectiveness depends on the preparedness of the mind, body, and spirit of the person doing the meditation.

You will not be on Olympic monk-level meditation on your first try or even your first few tries. For meditation to be effective, you have to prepare your mind by accepting full responsibility for your life and seeing that your actions will always be what you have control over. That is the key to unlocking the world you want to build for yourself. So you must have full confidence in the action of meditation because it will help you unlock the power in you, the power that will help you improve your understanding of self, decrease your attachment, give you a sense of purpose, reduce your ego, increase your level of consciousness and your self-awareness.

You will ultimately start to see the world as it is rather than as you think it is, and you will begin to take action to shape your world as you envision it to be. You will be in a state of peaceful happiness and still be ambitious as fuck.

Listen, I know meditation can be super boring. If you have ever tried to meditate and you did not enjoy it, it's probably because you were trying a meditation technique that I believe is frankly outdated or perfect if you lived on a mountain and meditated under a mango tree. The type of meditation that involves "the stillness of the mind". That type of meditation is boring, it is hard to maintain, and often makes you feel anxious when you miss a meditation session. I totally agree that it is not for everyone. Especially anyone that is just starting out. Did I mention it is hard? The reason for this difficulty is because your mind is not designed to make you happy. Your mind is designed to keep you alive, and because of that, it is always busy and thinking, plus, we live in the 21st Century. We have the internet, social media, cars, planes, AI, machine learning, robots, etc. The point is: you have a lot of stuff going on, and you cannot be expected to meditate the same way Buddhist monks meditated 100 years ago. In this chapter, you will learn a new way to meditate that will not bore you or make you feel bad even if you miss a day or two - just like you wouldn't feel bad for having a rest day or two if you were training your muscles for the Olympics or whatever competition you'd be preparing for because rest is good.

The type of meditation you will learn will help you train the mind more quickly by allowing you to flex your mental muscles. The objectives of meditation involve calming the mind, observing your thoughts and emotions, and centering our thoughts, and focusing on a single intention. An example will be to focus on the face of a loved one for about 5 minutes if you were performing a visual type of meditation, and you want to cultivate feelings of love and connection.

The objectives come with long-term benefits way after you have finished meditating. You will have gained:

FINDING HAPPINESS IN THE FACE OF SUFFERING

- A calm mind
- clarity
- emotional resilience
- self-awareness
- creativity
- confidence
- kindness
- charisma
- increased luck
- and happiness

Studies have shown that meditation decreases anxiety and depression. I can personally testify to the anxiety part. Meditation was one of the things that helped me overcome my anxiety. The good thing about technology is that we can measure the effects of meditation. It is thus easy to test the benefits of the newer, more exciting ways of meditating. I can testify to the meditation's impact because I felt like I was high on happy drugs for at least the first two months of my initiation into meditating religiously for a minimum of 5 days a week for about 15 to 30 minutes at a time.

The new meditation methods, which are just as effective as the outdated meditation, involve the same technique that the top sportsmen and women use to train their minds. This is through visualisation. Visualisation is a technique where you form a mental image of something. During visualisation, you picture yourself doing things or in situations and couple this picture with smell, touch, and emotions. When you use visualisation techniques, you harness the power of your subconscious mind.

Like I mentioned earlier, I also tried the outdated meditation, and I failed at it. (1), because I hadn't learned how to breathe, and (2), because I hadn't yet done my base work on myself to fully take responsibility for my life and be grateful for everything in it. I really tried to keep to it for about 2 weeks, but I was new, and it was so dull, I preferred to face whatever the world threw at me than to have to do meditation. I basically quit for about 6 months until I had done the base work on my mind to learn and understand why I was unhappy and found a newer, better way to meditate. When I found out the more modern way of meditation and kept at it, I felt relaxed and energetic at the same time.

Meditation changes our brainwaves. When we are relaxed and ready to meditate, our alpha brain waves rise. Alpha brain waves are dominant during quietly flowing thoughts and in some meditative states. Our alpha brain waves also rise in-between twilight times when we are very relaxed but not asleep. Alpha is "the power of now", being here, in the present. Alpha is the resting state of the brain. Alpha waves aid overall mental coordination, calmness, alertness, mind/body integration, and learning. Monks with Olympic-level mediation skills that have been meditating for years can easily activate their alpha brain waves in a second.

FINDING HAPPINESS IN THE FACE OF SUFFERING

The real science and magic with meditation are how it affects our happiness and our Gamma brainwaves. The high peak of Gamma brainwaves is seen during states of joy. An author that best describes the effect of meditation is Daniel Goleman. I will let you read what he said, without changes from the Big Think video on YouTube. He explained the remarkable brainwaves of high-level meditators.

Here's what Daniel Goleman said:

"My co-author of the book Altered Traits is a neuroscientist, Richard Davidson. He has a lab at the University of Wisconsin. It's a very large lab, has dedicated scanners, and has about 100 people working there. He was able to do some remarkable research where he flew Olympic-level meditators—who live in Nepal or India typically. Some in France—he flew them over to the lab and put them through a protocol in his brain scanners and did state-of-the-art tests and the results were just astounding. We found, for example, or he found that their brain waves are really different. Perhaps the most remarkable findings in the Olympic-level meditators have to do with their gamma wave. All of us get the Gamma wave for a very short period when we solve a problem we've been grappling with, even if it's something that's vexed us for months. We get about half a second of Gamma; it's the strongest wave in the electroencephalogram (EEG) spectrum. We get it when we bite into an apple or imagine biting into an apple. For a brief period, a split-second, inputs from the taste, sound, smell, vision, all of that come together in that imagined bite into the apple. But that lasts a very short period in an ordinary EEG.

What was stunning was that the Olympic-level meditators, these are people who have done up to 62,000 lifetime hours of meditation. Their brainwave shows gamma very strong all the time as a lasting trait no matter what they're doing. It's not a state effect, it's not during their meditation alone, but it's just their everyday state of mind."

He continues...

"We actually have no idea what that means experientially. Science has never seen it before. We also find that in these Olympic level meditators when we asked them, for example, to do a meditation on compassion, their level of gamma jumps 700 to 800 percent in a few seconds. This has also never been seen by science. So we have to assume that the special state of consciousness you see in the highest-level meditators is a lot like something described in the classical meditation literature centuries ago. Which is that there is a state of being which is not like our ordinary state. Sometimes it's called liberation, enlightenment, awake, whatever the word may be, we suspect there's really no vocabulary that captures what that might be. The people that we've talked to in this Olympic level group say, 'it's very spacious and you're wide open, you're prepared for whatever may come' - we just don't know. But we do know it's quite remarkable."

Imagine living in a state of openness to whatever may come without worry or fear. A state of acceptance and without clinging to outcomes. With visual meditation, you can get your gamma brainwaves to spike when getting the mental images. Better yet, if you immerse all your senses to touch, taste and smell. The longer and more often you do this, the calmer and blissful you will become. You will become a whole lot more mindful, more satisfied, and at peace. Personally, it took me a month to realise I no longer had anxiety. I'm not really sure when my anxiety disappeared, but I just noticed one day that I no longer had anxiety. It was less than a month from the day I started my visual meditation. My depression lifted in the same week I started. Yes, only a week. I was able to properly manage situations that would have otherwise stressed me out through mindful emotional resilience. I was in a space where I would typically be stressed because I was still heavily indebted. I got phone calls every other day from debt collectors. Instead of stressing, I actually embraced the situation and got to know my collectors, and even started to have pleasant, friendly conversations with them. I gained clarity to a lot of the things that stressed me out because look, at the end of the day, the question I always asked myself was: "what is the worst that could happen?". Funnily, that was the most calming question I ever asked myself. This one question of "what is the worst that could happen?" is also based on stoicism.

So, yeah, the new meditation technique meant for our busy minds and current times does not take thirty minutes to one hour. It does not require sitting in a pure, lucid state of mind as most people think. Yes, it will give you the exact same benefits, and this new meditation technique could take you five minutes to ten minutes a day. You can get the exact benefits that monks get from the old meditation techniques through visual meditation techniques.

"Just because you are going through difficult times does not mean you can't be happy. The only setback is that your mind focuses on survival, not your happiness as per its natural function. However, it is your job to train your mind to focus on the things that bring you joy." @Waleadejumo via Twitter

Reason to Meditate Daily:

When you want to get physically stronger, do you just work out once or do you do it repeatedly? The answer is: you do it repeatedly. And when you stop doing your workout, you start to lose muscle and get weaker. The same goes for meditation. Meditation is the workout for the mind. When you meditate, you have to do it daily in order to keep the mind trained. You do not have to sit and meditate; you can walk and meditate, you can do workouts such as Qi gong and meditate, you can do yoga and meditate, etc. When you become mentally stronger, you need to continue your meditation, otherwise, you will get mentally weaker. Reading this book is like reading a book about doing workouts. The book is only a seed. You will not get stronger by reading about working out unless you actually do the workouts yourself. Similarly, you will not get mentally stronger just by reading this book.

Imagine you are planting a seed. This seed you have planted is a seed of hope, and for this seed to germinate and the plant to grow, you will need to water it daily. This book is a deep seed of hope that has gone deep into your subconscious. Its job is to weed your mind, tilt the soil, and plant a seed. Now, this seed that has been planted needs to be watered daily.

FINDING HAPPINESS IN THE FACE OF SUFFERING

Now picture yourself watering that seed of hope. What does that look like to you? Is it enough that you have read this book? No! The mind is one of the most resilient "organs" in the body. The mind is powerful, and it takes some time for the brain to truly unlearn old ways. To test how resilient the mind is to being rewired, Destin Sandlin, founder of Smarter Every Day performed an experiment called the "Unlearning Challenge - The Backwards Brain Bicycle".

He created an educational video on YouTube where he demonstrates just how difficult it is for an adult to truly unlearn something.

Link: The Backwards Brain Bicycle - Smarter Every Day 133[1]

In the video, Destin Sandlin is confronted with a challenge when his engineers tweak a bicycle so that when he turns the handlebars to the left, it makes him go right and vice versa. He thought it'd be easy – as easy as riding an ordinary bicycle. But he was wrong…

After a series of frustrating attempts (captured in the video), Sandlin concluded that knowledge is not the same as understanding and just having the information does not mean that you have the expertise. So, although he finally did manage to learn to ride the bike a few months later, it was after many failed attempts.

---

1. https://www.youtube.com/watch?v=MFzDaBzBlL0&ebc=ANyPxKqwBf7-hmSyIGIj1FdIfNTIkL_Ed_KLT2igkSEvaPo3xO0WxwgPvsK6WdRvth4DiWaKjGE6zD9ULoQXcZ_mbS1bI19J8A

This bike, and the many failed attempts of many of his workshop participants to learn how to ride it, also illustrate how our brain tricks us into thinking the same way (bias). It showed that the more rigid our thinking, the more difficult it can be to change, even when we want to.

This is why it can be difficult to unlearn something as an adult – kids are usually better at this. Destin's son was given the same challenge of learning to ride the backward brain bicycle, and he mastered it in less than half the time it took Destin. Destin's son showed us there is a lesson to be learned.

And the lesson is that we need to be aware of and question how we interpret the world around us. We must also realise that knowledge on its own is not enough, we need the attitudes and skills, which come after lots of practice and effort and from seeing things from different perspectives.

So what happened when Destin jumped on a "normal" bike months later? He could not ride a regular bike. He had reprogrammed his brain's body memory to do things in a new way.

This is what happens to your mind when you meditate every day and fall into a routine habit. This process is called the watering and weeding process. You don't stop it even when the seed has germinated into a plant.

That seed of hope can only be taken care of by watering it every day through meditation and through a set of well-planned routines. I am telling you this because too many people read, but they do not practice. The practice is how we build the

FINDING HAPPINESS IN THE FACE OF SUFFERING

attitudes and the skills written about in this book, which can be done through a daily meditation practice. Meditation can be performed at any time of the day, but I have found that performing it first thing in the morning is best because it sets the tone for your day and is primed to go forth and have an amazing day.

- How do you meditate?

See the steps below to learn how. I will focus on visual meditation as it is the fastest and the most effective form of meditation, it only requires a few minutes each day to perform and it has been proven to be very effective with reprogramming the mind and evolving the brain.

- Visual meditation

Step 1: We will focus on Compassion

First, sit comfortably upright with your eyes closed or unfocused, breathe in, and exhale slowly, focusing on your breath. Count to 4 while you slowly inhale, hold your breath for 4 seconds and count to 4 while you slowly exhale and repeat.

As thoughts race through your mind, don't actively try to ignore them. Rather let them float by, without attaching to any particular one. If you find yourself distracted, bring your focus to your breathing. See the air flowing into your nose and down your pipe, into your lungs.

Bring your focus to your eyelids and relax them. Relax your jaw and your shoulders. When you are sufficiently relaxed, think of someone who makes you happy. Focus on your altruistic love for them.

We all have unconditional love for a child or someone dear. Someone that you feel only intentions of goodwill towards. Such moments of love usually last ten, fifteen seconds, one minute, then we'd do something else, we go about our work. But suppose you take that beautiful, strong warm feeling, and instead of letting it disappear after fifteen seconds, you cultivate it. For five, ten minutes, by reliving it. Coming back if you are distracted, keeping the clarity - the vividity of that.

And that's it. After practicing that simple meditation exercise, you can begin to spread that compassionate feeling to other specific people, strangers around you, a particular part of the world, or the world as a whole.

The mind reacts to this type of meditation, and the brain actually develops a stronger capability for emotional control.

Step 2: Gratitude

The next step while in your meditative state is to think about three things in your life that you can be grateful for. It helps to write down these things before you start your meditations when you are just starting out. The things you can be grateful for can be your positive experiences from the day before, home, car, family, yourself, the gifts you have, the job you have, your wonderful colleagues, your neighbours, your neighbourhood, anything that you bought for yourself, working from home

FINDING HAPPINESS IN THE FACE OF SUFFERING

versus sitting in traffic to get to work every day, etc. The list can go on.

In this meditative state, you only need to think about three things in your personal life, three things in your work life, and three things about yourself. In your meditative state, you must visualise these things when they happened. For example, when you bought your car, the smell of the car, the joy you felt, and the smiles you had. The same goes for anything, whether it is your home, cell phone, a book, a new mug, new shoes, etc. You need to remember and experience the time that thing brought you that initial joyous feeling before you got used to having it in your life. Walk your senses through the feelings and then move to the next meditation step.

Step 3: Forgiveness

In this step, you need to practice letting go of situations causing you pain and suffering. It is also useful to write down the names of anyone that has hurt you and write down situations you were hurt by. This can be something recent or something from a long time ago. It is never too early or too late to forgive someone or a situation.

In this step, you want to only focus on one person or one situation at a time because you can repeat this step the following day and keep forgiving people and situations each day as you grow. In this step, you must visualise the face of the person you want to forgive and see them right in front of you, then remember and feel the pain and hurt you felt because of the situation you were in with this person. Then take a deep breath in, and say out loud to this person, "I forgive you, and I ask that you forgive me." Then breathe out, and while you breathe out, release any anger and pain you felt towards this person. Feel the negative emotion leave your body and picture this person now saying to you, "I forgive you, and I ask that you forgive me too".

Repeat this step as many times as you need and for as many days, weeks, and months as you need to completely heal and let go of any anger and pain a person or a situation has caused you.

Step 4: Your vision

Knowing what you are working towards and having a clear vision and meditating on it trains your subconscious to keep your actions aligned with this vision. In this step, you must visualise what your ideal life looks like in the next 3 to 5 years. See yourself living this life. See yourself getting an award for living this life. Hear the cheers from people congratulating you for this achievement. Picture the smells of this life and picture yourself being content with this life. When you visualise this life, you increase your vibrations towards this life. Take a moment to enjoy this life.

Step 5: Short-term goals.

Now picture the steps you will take today or tomorrow to ensure that you have a fantastic day—a day filled with joy, progress, good health for both your mind and body. Picture what you will do from the time you wake up, making your bed, drinking a glass of water, meditating, exercising, having breakfast, going to work, working on a project, reading a book, talking to your loved ones, getting a good night's sleep, etc. Plan your entire day in this step, and for each step of the plan, say to yourself, "wouldn't it be nice to [fill in the gap] here with whatever it is you will do for that part of your day".

This visual way of planning your day ensures that you start your day relaxed and with a plan. Sometimes, your day will not go as you planned it, which is okay, but you will follow through much easier. This visualisation step will help you build routines and habits in your life, which will help you achieve your goals of being happier, and other goals. You have to carry out the actions you have set out for yourself in this step throughout your day.

Step 6: Energy

In this step, you want to align your energy to your actions and vision. You can pray to God or your ancestors for guidance, strength, and courage to take the action steps and to always do the right thing, and then lock in the belief that you have what it takes to go on with your day and make your vision a reality. If you do not believe in God and ancestors, you can picture a light swirling inside you and travelling from your chest to your abdomen, spreading to every part of your body, cleansing your energy, spirit and then locking in this light to give you strength and courage to make the right decisions; giving you the power to go on and carry out the vision you have created for yourself and your day.

Learn As Much As Possible

When we are born, we are like a brand-new computer. It is loaded with software that allows it to function. Over the years, this computer's software is continuously upgraded; this is us when we are born as babies. Our brains are the hard drive, our knowledge the software. Our software gets outdated and often needs to be upgraded. In order for our brains to form new meaningful thoughts, we have to add meaningful things to them, which is where reading comes in.

Warren Buffet, Oprah Winfrey and Bill gates all recommend spending at least 5 hours a week reading personal development non-fiction books. Personal development in the awakened state happens through a proactive process. Warren Buffett is an American business magnate, investor, and philanthropist, the chairman and CEO of Berkshire Hathaway. He is considered one of the most successful investors in the world. He has a net worth of US$88.9 billion as of December 2019, and he has been quoted saying that he still spends five to six hours a day reading. "Everybody can read what I read, it is a level playing field," Buffett used to tell his late wife, Susan Buffett. Let that sink in.

"And he loves that because he is competitive," Susan said of Buffett. "He's sitting there all by himself in his office, reading these things that everybody else can read, but he loves the idea that he is going to win."

Mark Cuban, an American entrepreneur and investor, echoes the same sentiment. "Everything I read was public," he writes. "Anyone could buy the same books and magazines. The same information was available to Anyone who wanted it. Turns out most people didn't want it."

This means that you can read the same things the most successful people in the world are reading and apply the same knowledge they are gaining to apply to your business and your life.

I used to find reading so painful. If you had asked me to choose between reading a book on personal development and death, I would have hesitated and had to think about the answer before choosing to read. To be honest, I was also arrogant and believed that hard work was all I needed to succeed. I used to think that programming, marketing, digital marketing, and other challenging skills was what I needed to make it in life. I was wrong.

My life started to change when I took reading advice from my business partner. The first book he recommended to me was called the E-myth Revisited by Michael E. Gerber. If you wonder what the founders of some of the world's best businesses, such as McDonald's, the burger company, did to create and grow their franchise businesses, you will want to read this book. If you want to walk away from your company for up to 3 months and not have things fall apart, you definitely want to read this book.

FINDING HAPPINESS IN THE FACE OF SUFFERING

I am quite competitive, so reading brought me up to the same playing field as my leading business peers. It also helped me gain knowledge that I would not have otherwise had. It also quickly started to erase any sense of inadequacy or the sense of imposter syndrome that I had. Imposter syndrome is a psychological pattern in which an individual doubts their skills, talents, or accomplishments. This doubt has a persistent internalised fear of being exposed as a fraud. As I read more and more, I gained more confidence in my work, my accomplishments, and I understood my failures. Reading gave me a genuine ability to understand where I had gone wrong and where I was going to go wrong.

It is only through the action of reading that you will be able to truly grow faster than the world around you. This is something smart people know. Please note that leisure fiction reading does not count. Reading fiction for entertainment does not develop your interpersonal and intrapersonal skills. Who reads? Reading is done by great CEOs, extraordinary people, students of life itself and employees in workplaces that excel faster than you can imagine.

If you ever wondered why someone just keeps moving forward in bounds and you're not, it's because they are probably investing time in their minds by reading. Yes, they fucking read! Just like you are reading this book right now. At work and with friends, I often get asked for a book recommendation, I almost always recommend the book by Dale Carnegie: How to Win Friends and Influence People because it is a brilliant book to improve your interpersonal skills.

How to Win Friends and Influence People is a self-help book written by Dale Carnegie, published in 1936. Over 15 million copies have been sold worldwide, making it one of the best-selling books of all time. In 2011, it was number 19 on Time Magazine's list of the 100 most influential books. This is because books like these are based on interpersonal development and apply to us even today. You can attain knowledge that millions of excelling people have learned because it is a level playing field regarding reading. These books will teach you "how-to", but the rest will lay with you.

Learning the "How to" is just the first step. Knowledge is nothing without practical application. In my case, I applied the knowledge gained in this book in my business and with my friends to test the results. What happened? I started to see an improvement in my leadership skills because my circle of influence became stronger just by thinking of an outcome before acting and remembering to make everyone feel important and appreciated. I served with intent, and I intended to make others feel important. Of course, we know this is important, however, when you read a book with examples and scenarios, it starts to help you make connections in your mind when things have not gone your way. You start to see how and why aspects of your life are just not working out. An awakening starts to take place.

Reading is not just done by billionaires. Yes, I know I dropped a few billionaire names but only because they are famous and role models to millions of people. Look, we can't all be billionaires, but we can be better and keep on improving certain aspects of our lives. So what should you be doing? You should be reading at least 5 hours a week because it ensures that you will keep improving and get better for your goals. This is also a Kaizen approach which helps to evolve the mind. This 5-hour reading per week rule is so effective that some of the more forward-thinking companies make it part of their employees' work time.

You should look at learning the way you look at exercise. Lifelong exercise is good, as is lifelong learning. You need to move past the cliche that all you need to excel is certificates and realise that you need to do a minimum amount of learning in your life each day to have and sustain a successful career. Just as we have minimum recommended dosages of vitamins, steps per day, and aerobic exercise for leading a healthy life physically; we should be more rigorous about how we, as an information society, think about the minimum doses of deliberate learning for leading healthy lives economically.

The long-term effects of NOT learning are just as insidious as the long-term effects of not having a healthy lifestyle. In the Fourth Industrial Revolution time we live in today, those who do not spend at least 5 hours a week learning something new will soon find themselves replaced by technology.

You might believe that the more productive you are, the more successful you'll be. Although productivity plays a role in success, it's nothing without lifelong learning. If you're always focused on your current work, rather than on long-term self-improvement, you'll never see much development. It can be hard to allow yourself five hours a week for learning that doesn't come with an immediate reward, but you'll thank yourself for it in the long run. Try to look beyond your daily paycheck and dedicate time to becoming the best possible version of yourself instead.

Take inspiration from some of the world's most successful entrepreneurs and spend five hours a week on deliberate learning. You'll soon be lightyears ahead of your friends and colleagues, and well on your way to success.

Reading can be done either via eBooks with tablet devices or even your smartphone and computer with apps like Scribd. There are other applications out there, which you just need to search. You can also just buy a good old book and read the classical way. Personally, I do not enjoy reading hard copy books, but I know a lot of people who do. I prefer to listen to audiobooks. Audiobooks are an easy way to acquire any book, and the best part about most audiobooks is that you can listen to the book being read to you in the author's voice. Hence, it feels like you are being personally mentored by the author themselves. Some people may say that they prefer to listen to podcasts and my response usually is that, if you listen to podcasts, then you may enjoy audiobooks. There are several audiobook apps on the market. I personally use Scribd because of its very attractive price point of just $9.99 per month at the time of writing this book. With Scribd, you can listen to an unlimited number of audiobooks per month compared to paying for each book. Audiobooks saved my life.

It is up to each person to find and discover how you read a book but whatever you do, make sure to read. Your future and your success in the times we live in today depend on it. If I did not

FINDING HAPPINESS IN THE FACE OF SUFFERING

start being an avid reader, my life would have never changed. I might have still been a nice guy but a terrible leader, I would have remained unhappy. I would have continued working long, hard hours and kept failing, and I would have never written this book.

- I learned to read the hard way

Our human mind is not designed to make us happy and successful. Our human mind is designed to keep us alive; it is motivated to act based on two factors - pain and pleasure. As humans, we act because we want to move away from pain or move towards pleasure. Reading is not something most people gravitate towards, and I know this because reading was not pleasurable for years. I had to learn to read the right books the hard way. I had to go through a painful growth the hard way in my personal life. The pain I felt was so bad that the pain of reading became pleasurable compared to the pain I was in before I started to read.

In university, I was a track and field athlete. I was ranked number 1 in KwaZulu-Natal, a South African province with an 11.3 million population, for over 8 years I ranked in the top 3 in South Africa at some point. I went from this to starting a business and becoming a managing director of my company. My approach to growing the company was to learn as much of the hard skills needed to develop an online company, which resulted in the company growing pretty fast. Within just 3 years, I turned over millions of Rands per month and had a staff count of 15 people within a few years. Bear in mind that I had never had a real job and never been mentored. I had to learn many things about the business quickly, but I did not know I had to learn interpersonal growth skills. That was me. I thought self-help was lame. I thought reading books was a waste of time. I lived an unconscious life and did not know that I could learn how to be a happier person. I chased pleasure instead of peace of mind. I did not know some people can coach you about life. I thought I knew a lot, but I really knew only what I already knew and nothing more.

Do you know what's so common? People do not know that they can read and learn about being happy, being a better parent, how to be a better spouse, how to save money in a marriage, and how to live a life of peace, etc. The world is filled with such gaps in knowledge. It's either because of ignorance because we think we know or don't even know that such knowledge exists in books. I admit that I was a fool.

I thought I knew a lot, and I remember this lady I once spoke to, the former CEO of INOXA, saying to me to always stay humble. Boy,

Was she talking from experience?

It's so true that the world's most outstanding teachers are heartbreaks, empty pockets, and failures because it took all three for me to pick up books to read to improve my life skills.

Most of us think we know how things in life work, but we don't know jack unless we go and upgrade our knowledge from books like this. The world is filled with experts with an abundance of information due to the internet. Yet, people are just going through life like they have shit figured out when

FINDING HAPPINESS IN THE FACE OF SUFFERING

they don't, but do not take the initiative to pick up a damn book and read. The worst are those who argue with experts based on their knowledge from reading conspiracy theories on Facebook, Twitter, and other internet sources.

Let me ask you a question; how many books have you read in the past 6 months on personal development? I'm not talking about fiction. How many have you read in the past 6 months? If you follow the recommendation of 5 hours a week, then you should have read at least 25 books. However, I say screw that because you should be reading 8 hours a week. Ok, maybe 5 hours. Which is about how long it would take you to read this book.

Where do you get your information from? Do you get your information from reputable sources? Do you trust what experts say or do you believe anything you read on the internet? We live in a time where false information can be created to appear legitimate giving rise to flat earthers. If you don't know what a flat earther is, flat earthers are people that believe that the earth is flat, not round. These people believe that NASA and governments worldwide are conspiring to keep the real shape of the earth hidden from us. Let me just say that this is all bullshit and that the earth is somewhat round. My point is: get your knowledge and information from experts.

I read 1 - 3 short books a week sometimes. Reading for at least 5 hours is the recommendation for how much you should be reading if you really want to get to your goals a lot faster in life, so do yourself a favour. Pick up a book and make a habit of reading at least 2 books a month.

I will help with some recommendations of some timeless books that go as far back as 1926. Below is a list of some of the books I recommend:

- How to Win Friends and Influence People by Dale Carnegie

- 7 Habits of Highly Effective People by Stephen Covey

- 25 Habits of Highly Successful People by Stephan Schiffman (this book is great for anyone in business or if you have a job, or want to be good with sales, basically: for anyone who wants to be successful

- The E-Myth Revisited by Michael E. Gerber: If you are an entrepreneur, are starting a business, or already have a business where you have to micromanage, then read this book. I wish I had read this book sooner.

- The next book is especially great for leaders in an organisation. It's called Exponential Organisations: Why New Organisations are Ten Times Better, Faster, and Cheaper Than Yours (and what to Do About It) by Michael S. Malone, Salim Ismail, and Yuri van Geest.

- One fiction book I will recommend is The Richest Man in Babylon by George Samuel Claso. This book has fables on acquiring wealth, investing and how to use this money from your investments to fund your luxury lifestyles. I would, however, recommend that you pick up a book on proper investments after reading this book.

Reading is not just important for adults but children too. Studies have shown that children who learn to read early continue to get higher grades than their peers through grade school. Also, when children learn to read, they have greater general knowledge, expand their vocabulary, and become more fluent readers.

Remember, a person who does not read is as good as a person who cannot read. Similarly, knowledge without action is pointless. So put the knowledge you get from books into action.

- Parents in Leadership Positions but are Not Leaders

Do you know how a child would turn out if they were isolated in a dark room (provided with food, water, etc.) with no human contact until they were grown?

Unfortunately, we have practical, real-life data on what happens in this scenario. On November 4, 1970, in Los Angeles, United States of America, child welfare authorities discovered a girl named Genie who was isolated from everything at the age of 20 months.

When she was found at the age of 13, she became the subject of intense scientific studies. Researchers saw her as a goldmine of information to study human development. She notably was unable to talk (not really surprising). While she acquired some basic language skills during her care by the state of California, she quickly regressed when she started to hop from one adult mental care institution to the next. She also severely lacked development in everything that separates human beings from feral animals. Although she developed non-verbal skills quickly, she had no verbal communication skills and no hygienic abilities.

It is best to hope that such cases do not ever happen again.

This is a case of nature versus nurture. The characteristics of children are highly influenced by the environment they grow up in. In genetics, it is defined as the phenotype, which is a combination of one's genes with the environment.

The equation looks like this:

Genotype (aka genes) + environment = phenotype (characteristic)

We have the power to highly influence our own characteristics, and especially children during the vital stages of their development. Many parents raise their kids consciously, which results in them growing into conscious adults, however, the number of parents who apply unconscious parenting greatly outweighs the number of conscious parents in this world.

So, the question is: how are parents supposed to raise conscious kids and prepare them for adulthood when they themselves have not been raised to be prepared for adulthood? Most parents do not even know how to handle adult life or have control over their own lives. The great thing about the 21st century is that there are free sources of information to help children grow up consciously. However, there are paid sources such as the animated curated course for kids by leading children's educators such as Gahmya Drummond-Bey, founder of kid YOUniversity.

FINDING HAPPINESS IN THE FACE OF SUFFERING

Parents inherit a leadership position, but this does not make them inherent leaders because leaders are not born, they are created. And just because you are a dad, mum, uncle, aunt, or guardian does not make you a leader.

To be a leader, you need to work on yourself and develop leadership skills. Yes, it's skills that can be developed and can be learned. It doesn't happen once you have read a book but over time of applying leadership skills.

It might sound harsh to hear me tell you that what most of us think we know about leadership is inadequate, and what keeps us inadequate is our arrogance. To develop your leadership skills, you need to be curious. You need to continue to learn because you have just one brain vs 7.7 billion brains plus all the past human brains that have passed and left their knowledge. The fact is that in the greater scope of things, you know very little.

To lead effectively, never stop learning and practicing what you learn. Learn by picking up a book, attending seminars, going to masterclasses, follow accounts that add to your self-development on social media and work on your damn self so that we can raise a better society for the future.

ADEWALE ADEJUMO

Conclusion

You are responsible for your happiness. It is a choice, and it is entirely your responsibility. I have written this book to take you through the journey of the mindset of happy and successful people. Do you notice I did not write "Happy or successful"? This is because I am not separating either from each other in this book. If you want to achieve happiness and success combined, then the insights and teachings in this book should be followed.

I love the fact that you have read this book. It makes me confident that you are on the exact path that you need to be on to become an even happier version of yourself. It is okay to seek help if you require support; however, when it comes down to the work of healing and growing, that is 100% your responsibility.

Almost everyone extremely happy started from somewhere. You'll never be truly happy if you do not take steps to improve your state of happiness. Many people ACT happy and try to look happy instead of learning from the happiest people in the world and learning what those people's routines and habits are that make them happy and then rehearse those habits and routines every day. Those habits and routines come down to meditation to raise your consciousness and reprogram your mind. What is even more important is what you meditate upon. Meditating on love, kindness, gratitude, forgiveness, your purpose, your goals and your spirituality will guarantee you the level of awareness and changes within yourself that you need to become a content human being.

The habits described in this book are based on the patterns I formed and have had remarkable effects in changing my life and mindset.

I formed the habits because I made a decision that would change my life forever. That decision was that I did not want to be unhappy anymore. More accurately, I said to myself that "I want to be happy".

I was your classic unhappy person whose life seemed like a struggle, but I knew my life could be better.

One day, I woke up and decided that my life needed to be better, that it was time to be happy. I picked up one book after the other and then the other until I had read a ton of books on how to be happy and take control of my life.

Over the past few years of changing my mindset, reading, forming new habits, I became the happiest person I know. I have been blessed to be able to share this knowledge with you.

The teachings in this book have ultimately changed my entire life, career and purpose.

I had many possible titles for this book because frankly, I could have called it anything. Anything from "The Foundation of Happiness", "How to Hack Your Mind for Happiness", "Find Purpose and Happiness" to "Mind Happiness Hack". But you wouldn't have found this book or bought it, would you? So I went for a catchy title like "Finding Happiness in The Face

FINDING HAPPINESS IN THE FACE OF SUFFERING

of Suffering" but also because, for the first six months of practicing the teachings in this book, I felt like a totally different person from who I was before.

I have still faced life challenges. This book itself was a challenge. I massively and optimistically thought I would write it in a week (I'm laughing out loud as I just wrote that sentence), but it took over a year for me to finish it. It happened by taking a step forward at a time and having patience because patience "is knowing" that it will happen, and it has happened. Life will always have its challenges, and it won't be easy. However, our mindset to the challenges and our actions to them determine our level of happiness.

When you're done reading this book, you will hear two voices in your head. One voice will say, "This is not who I am because I'm a late sleeper. I'm not a morning person. I don't do routines. Etc". And the "other" voice will say "I need to change my mindset. I need to create my own happiness; I want to try the thoughts and ideas in this book out". Listen to the "other" voice and tell your friends to do the same. The other voice is the voice that led you to read this book in the first place. It is your spirit voice that is guiding you to where you want to be in your life. Also called your spirit guide.

I listened to the "other" voice. It has brought me happiness, and it has changed my entire life, career and purpose. It has led me to write this book and teach many people the lessons I have learned and developed to become the happiest version of yourself and principles to follow to take control of your life.

In my case, it has been gratifying, and I have no regrets. I am living the exact life that I visualised and planned. I started teaching my lessons to my colleagues, close friends, family and finally, my online community. I received very positive feedback, with some of my online followers even writing to encourage me to write a book. I would like to thank everyone that wrote to me because your feedback was very encouraging as I was already in the process of writing this book.

I wanted to make this book concise to make it easy for anyone to read and follow. Even those people that wouldn't ordinarily read a book on happiness. Storytelling is not my forte, but I aimed to bring clarity with actionable steps to gain control over your mind, body and spirit.

Whatever your inspiration was that caused you to pick up this book, I hope I have made it worth your while. Be happy like a Buddha and I don't mean to become Buddhist. It is a metaphor for you to live your life and take the lessons learned from hundreds of thousands of years from millions of brilliant minds and apply them to your life in the 21st century. It is a metaphor for you to live your life based on reality, the best way possible, and live to your real purpose and passion. It is a metaphor to let your happy inner child that was truly happy come out to play.

One of the reasons it took me long to finish this book was because I continued to learn new things every day. If I did not decide to put the pen down, I would still be writing this book today. However, you can continue to learn the lessons I am learning from myself and from the best life coaches, business

FINDING HAPPINESS IN THE FACE OF SUFFERING

coaches and entrepreneurs in the world by joining me on my Podcast - Happy Like Buddha at HappyLikeBuddha.com. Or on Google Podcast, Apple Podcast, Podbean, Stitcher, Pandora, and on Spotify.

Your mindset makes a huge difference in your happiness. Critics will tell you that happiness can be bought with money, and they are not wrong. The question is: how much happiness can money buy you? This book, perhaps and all the knowledge? However, the knowledge in this book means nothing unless you take action.

For the next 30 days, I want you to practice the visual meditation technique described in chapter 11 of this book. Your life will change, and it will only take 15 - 30 minutes of your day each day. It will help you form a better connection, let go of situations, focus on the abundance you already have, create life goals and accomplish them. It will change the way you see life and read books forever.

Most people may be tempted to stop the meditation when they start to feel great but let me ask you a question: do you only eat once? Or do you eat every day? I'm sure you eat every day. Likewise, you must continue to meditate every day because meditation is food for the mind. Your mind feeds on the food you give it. So, to keep your mind healthy, make sure you make meditation a part of your daily routine.

The beauty of Finding Happiness in The Face of Suffering is that the lessons can be applied to anyone at any age. You are never too old or too young for your mindset to shift and create a life true to yourself. No one is too old to start.

It takes only 30 days to shift your life. Heck, shorter for some people. I am sure that you have been on your journey of change for some time. The most important thing to do right now is to take action and to work on your happiness and not worry about it. You are where you need to be today. Now is your time to get started.

You are a creator. You can create the future you want through the power of your mind, desires and your actions. You are not stuck in the life you were born into or the culture of your tribe or your tradition. You are a compound of your habits and your routines, and you have the power to change who you are by changing your routine and your habits. Want to change your life? Then change your routine and your habits.

After my transformation from one of the most unhappy people I know, to becoming the happiest person I know, I said: "I know" because there are happier people than myself out there and I just don't know them yet. DM me if you are a happy person on my social media. I'd love to interview you and have a chat. Back to what I was saying, A statement I once read somewhere is, "we are all just spiritual beings having a human experience". This statement stuck with me because it gave me a different perspective of my own existence. Those remarks have compelled me to dive deeper into that statement which led me to pick up and read the Bhagavad Gita, a 5,153 year-old spiritual book.

FINDING HAPPINESS IN THE FACE OF SUFFERING

The Gita is set as a narrative dialogue between a man named Arjuna and Krishna in which a broad range of spiritual topics was covered. A lesson from the Gita was that humans have full control of the physical realm and that we are the creators of our own futures through the fruits of our actions. Positive actions create a positive response, and negative actions create a negative response. This is the law of the universe that governs us in both the physical and spiritual realms because there is energy in everything; in and around you. Your physical body is encapsulated in an energy field which is also referred to as your spirit. Your body is in your spirit and not the other way around.

The work from Jeffery Allen, who is a world-renowned energy healer and teacher shows how your energy is encapsulating your physical body and how you can work with your energy. This type of work shows how limitless our abilities are to achieve anything we want. Don't let your journey on becoming a happier and more enlightened human end here with this book. Your purpose should be your ultimate guide because those who are guided by their purpose are happier. They always have something to do, they have something to live and hope for.

Being purpose-driven and having a purpose-driven mindset will mean that your work will never truly be complete and will help you with a mastery of yourself and your craft.

A purpose-driven person only has to master one thing - themselves.

ADEWALE ADEJUMO

If after you finish this book, you still have questions you want to ask me, you can send me a message on my social media. My social media handles are:

Instagram: @therealwaleadejumo

Facebook: Adewaleadejumopage

Twitter: @waleadejumo

TikTok: @therealwaleadejumo

I read all messages and I do respond.

Your happiness starts with the thoughts you choose; the decisions you make and the actions you take. No one can do these for you, but you.

Choose positive thoughts through gratitude and you'll start to shift your focus on what is not there to the abundance of what is there. Choose forgiveness; to let go of situations that hurt you because it is wholly done and has gone and out of your control. Make sure to hold people accountable for their actions and don't be afraid to say NO.

When happy, you'll ultimately still be the same person. What will set you apart before and after are: your thoughts, routines, and your habits. Therefore, ensure you feed your mind with new ideas by reading books, develop methods that compliment your life in a way that makes it better and create good healthy habits.

FINDING HAPPINESS IN THE FACE OF SUFFERING

Your happiness is a process, and it is entirely your responsibility.

The fastest and easiest way to become happier is by taking time every day to appreciate the things you have and stop worrying about the things you don't have.

Thank you for reading Finding Happiness in The Face Suffering till the end. If this book has touched you, please send me an email at wale@adewaleadejumo.com. I cannot promise to reply to every email, but I promise to read every email. I am touched by the messages and the experiences you share, and I love reading words from every reader.

And please come and visit me on my website at adewaleadejumo.com. Now, go practice, teach and share the experiences and knowledge from this book with your friends and family. My friends, be Happy Like a Buddha.

ADEWALE ADEJUMO

Sources

Introduction

Depression Is Your Avatar Telling You It's Tired of Being .... (Accessed February 2020). https://jessishawaii.medium.com/depression-is-your-avatar-telling-you-its-tired-of-being-the-character-you-are-trying-to-play-ecc186ff8397

Hagen, G. (2003). Buddhism Is Not What You Think: Finding Freedom Beyond Beliefs

Likhiani, V. (2016). The Code of the Extraordinary Mind: 10 Unconventional Laws to Redefine Your Life and Succeed On Your Own Terms.

Tolle, E. (2001). The power of now.

Wheal, J. and Kotler, S. (2017). Stealing Fire: How Silicon Valley, the Navy SEALs, and Maverick Scientists Are Revolutionizing the Way We Live and Work

Take Responsibility

Beck, C. (2016). The Power of Ho'oponopono: An Introduction to the Ancient Hawaiian Healing Ritual

Covey, S. (1989). The 7 Habits of Highly Effective People

Hagen, G. (2003). Buddhism Is Not What You Think: Finding Freedom Beyond Beliefs

Holiday, R. (2016). Ego Is the Enemy

Sanei, J. (2017). What's Your Moonshot?: Future-proof yourself and your business in the age of exponential disruption

Watts, A. (1940). The Meaning of Happiness

Live Your Own Principle

Epictetus, (c. 55 - 135 AD). How to Be Free: An Ancient Guide to the Stoic Life

Jives, F. (2018). Stoicism: Guide to the Art of Ancient Stoic Philosophy

Manson, M. (2016). The Subtle Art of Not Giving a F*ck

Vitale, J. (2011). Instant Manifestation: The Real Secret to Attracting What You Want Right Now (Your Coach in a Box) Audio CD

Wright, R. (2017). Why Buddhism Is True

Experience Joy In The Face of Suffering

Beck, C. (2016). The Power of Ho'oponopono: An Introduction to the Ancient Hawaiian Healing Ritual

Dispenza, J. (2008). Evolve Your Brain: The Science of Changing Your Mind

Hanh, T. (2017). The Art of Living: Peace and Freedom in the Here and Now

Moffitt, P. (2008). Dancing with Life: Buddhist Insights for Finding Meaning and Joy in the Face of Suffering

Naim, R. (2016). The Art of Letting Go

Tolle, E. (1997). The Power of Now: A Guide to Spiritual Enlightenment

Tolle, E. (1999). Practicing the Power of Now

Live In A State Of Abundance

Barton, A., Futris, T. and Nielsen, R. (2015). Linking financial distress to marital quality: The

intermediary roles of demand/withdraw and spousal

gratitude expressions. The University of Georgia.

FINDING HAPPINESS IN THE FACE OF SUFFERING

Beck, C. (2016). The Secret Law of Attraction: Ask, Believe, Receive

Carnegie, Dale. (1936). How to win friends and influence people. How to stop worrying and start living

Cavaness, R. (2018). The Gratitude Effect: Shift Your Mindset, Optimize Your Outcomes, and Boost Emotional Well-Being

Covey, S. (1989). The 7 Habits of Highly Effective People

Dopamine deficiency: Symptoms, causes, and treatment. (Accessed June, 2020). https://www.medicalnewstoday.com/articles/320637

Honda, K. (2019). Happy Money: The Japanese Art of Making Peace with Your Money

Reklau, M. (2018). The Life-Changing Power of Gratitude: 7 Simple Exercises that will Change Your Life for the Better.

Tan, C. (2016). Joy on Demand: The Art of Discovering the Happiness Within

The Benefits of Gratitude: 6 Ways it Rewires Your Brain & Body. (Accessed June, 2020). https://www.consciouslifestylemag.com/benefits-of-gratitude-research/

Owning Less Means Having More

Jay, F. (2010). The Joy of Less: A Minimalist Guide to Declutter, Organize, and Simplify

Babauta, L. (2009). The Simple Guide to a Minimalist Life

Quote by Lao Tzu: "He who knows he has enough is rich .... (Accessed February, 2020). https://www.goodreads.com/quotes/141330-he-who-knows-he-has-enough-is-rich-perseverance-is

The Power Of Habits

Allen, D. (2001). Getting Things Done

Clear, J. (2018). Atomic Habits: An Easy & Proven Way to Build Good Habits & Break Bad Ones

Dalio, R. (2017). Principles: Life and Work

Duhigg, C. (2012). The Power of Habit

Ecker, T. (2005). Secrets of the Millionaire Mind: Mastering the Inner Game of Wealth (Abridged)

The Habit Loop | Habitica Wiki | Fandom. (Accessed March, 2020). https://habitica.fandom.com/wiki/The_Habit_Loop

Keller, G. and Papasan, J. (2012). The ONE Thing: The Surprisingly Simple Truth About Extraordinary Results

Schiffman, S. (1991). The 25 Sales Habits of Highly Successful People

Vanderkam, L. (2012). What the Most Successful People Do Before Breakfast: How to Achieve More at Work and at Home

Set Long-Term Goals

Hill, N. (1937). Think and Grow Rich

Horowitz, M. (2017). Awakened Mind: How Thoughts Become Reality

Lamott, A. (1994). Bird by Bird

Penn, J. (2016). The Successful Author Mindset: A Handbook for Surviving the Writer's Journey

Penn, J. (2018). How To Write Non-Fiction: Turn Your Knowledge Into Words

Ramsey, T. (2018). Mindset of the Successful: 7 Powerful and Highly Effective Success Habits Used by Millionaires to Attract Money, Wealth, Growth, and Achieve Life Mastery

FINDING HAPPINESS IN THE FACE OF SUFFERING

Something To Do

Akdeniz, C. (2016). Kaizen Philosophy Explained

Greene, R. (2012). Mastery

Johnson, V. (2013). How To Write a Book This Weekend, Even If You Flunked English Like I Did

Lamott, A. (1996). Word by Word

Miralles, F. and Garcia, H. (2016). Ikigai: The Japanese Secret to a Long and Happy Life

Roth, B. (2015). The Achievement Habit: Stop Wishing, Start Doing, and Take Command of Your Life

Vaynerchuk, G. (2018). Crushing It!: How Great Entrepreneurs Build Their Business and Influence-and How You Can, Too

Willink, T. (2019). The Science of Self Confidence: Develop an Unshakeable Self Esteem, Self Love and Self Confidence + Why You Need to Take Extreme Ownership for Your Self Confidence

Xue, M. (2018). Ikigai: The Japanese Secret Philosophy for a Happy Healthy Long Life With Joy and Purpose Every Day

Yoga: Fight stress and find serenity - Mayo Clinic. (Accessed July 2020). https://www.mayoclinic.org/healthy-lifestyle/stress-management/in-depth/yoga/art-20044733

Meditation

Best, J. and Best, R. (2017). Brain Apps: Hacking Neuroscience To Get There

Goleman, D. and Davidson, R. (2017). Altered Traits: Science Reveals How Meditation Changes Your Mind, Brain, and Body

Hargrave, J. (2016). Mind Hacking: How to Change Your Mind for Good in 21 Days

Jives, F. (2018). Stoicism: Guide to the Art of Ancient Stoic Philosophy

Likhiani, V. (2016). The Code of the Extraordinary Mind: 10 Unconventional Laws to Redefine Your Life and Succeed On Your Own Terms.

Proctor, B. (1984). You Were Born Rich

Shetty, J. (2020). Think Like a Monk

The Backwards Brain Bicycle - Smarter Every Day 133. https://www.youtube.com/watch?v=MFzDaBzBlL0&ebc=ANyPxKqwBf7-hmSyIGIj1FdIfNTIkL_Ed_KLT2igkSEvaPo3xO0WxwgPvsK6WdRvth

FINDING HAPPINESS IN THE FACE OF SUFFERING

Learn As Much As Possible

Anderson, C. (2016). TED Talks: The Official TED Guide to Public Speaking

Bill Gates: This is the key to Warren Buffett's success. (Accessed March 2020). https://www.cnbc.com/2019/06/03/bill-gates-this-is-the-key-to-warren-buffetts-success.html

Bill Gates, Warren Buffett And Oprah All Use The 5-Hour .... (Accessed March 2020). http://michaeldsimmons.com/bill-gates-warren-buffett-and-oprah-all-use-the-5-hour-rule/

Robbins, A. (1991). Awaken the Giant Within

Carnegie, Dale. (1936). How to win friends and influence people. How to stop worrying and start living

Covey, S. (1989). The 7 Habits of Highly Effective People

Dispenza, J. (2008). Evolve Your Brain: The Science of Changing Your Mind

Gerber, M. (1986). The E Myth

How the '5-Hours Rule' will make you successful? - Global .... (Accessed March 2020). https://www.globalvillagespace.com/how-the-5-hours-rule-will-make-you-successful/

Imposter Syndrome in the Art World — StudioGwyneth. (Accessed March 2020). https://www.gwynethmanley.com/sg-blog/2020/11/13/imposter-syndrome

Malone, M., Ismail, S., and Van Geest, Y. (2014). Exponential Organizations: Why New Organizations are Ten Times Better, Faster, and Cheaper Than Yours (and what to Do about It)

Clason, G. (1926). The Richest Man in Babylon

Starved, tortured, forgotten: Genie, the feral child who .... (Accessed August 2020). https://www.theguardian.com/society/2016/jul/14/genie-feral-child-los-angeles-researchers

Summary of How to Win Friends & Influence People by Dale .... (Accessed March 2020). https://www.overdrive.com/media/5396140/summary-of-how-to-win-friends-influence-people-by-dale-c

Warren Buffett - Wikipedia. (Accessed March 2020). https://en.wikipedia.org/wiki/Warren_Buffett

Warren Buffett and Mark Cuban agree: Reading is key to success. (Accessed March 2020). https://www.cnbc.com/2017/11/15/warren-buffett-and-mark-cuban-agree-reading-is-key-to-success.html

Willink, T. (2019). Growth Mindset: 7 Secrets to Destroy Your Fixed Mindset and Tap into Your Psychology of Success with Self Discipline, Emotional Intelligence and Self Confidence

Conclusion

Bach, D. (2019). The Latte Factor: Why You Don't Have to Be Rich to Live Rich

Chopra, D. (1994). The Seven Spiritual Saws of Success: A Practical Guide to the Fulfillment of y=Dour Dreams

Covey, S. (1989). The 7 Habits of Highly Effective People

Emerson, R. and Horowitz, M. (2014). Mastery of Life: The Self-Help Classics of Ralph Waldo Emerson. Audio book.

Hawley, J. (2001). The Bhagavad Gita: A Walkthrough for Westerners

Don't miss out!

Visit the website below and you can sign up to receive emails whenever Adewale Adejumo publishes a new book. There's no charge and no obligation.

https://books2read.com/r/B-A-BJCR-IAAUB

BOOKS 2 READ

Connecting independent readers to independent writers.

About the Author

Adewale Adejumo is an entrepreneur, podcast host and writer who knows what it feels like to come close to the edge. A man devoted to helping people have breakthroughs so that they can master their ability to take control of their lives. His insights into the fine line between happiness and suffering come from experience and learning from hundreds of personal growth experts around the world.

Read more at www.adewaleadejumo.com.

www.ingramcontent.com/pod-product-compliance
Lightning Source LLC
Chambersburg PA
CBHW072003290426
44109CB00018B/2116